Judicial Jurisdiction

Recent Titles in
Reference Guides to the United States Constitution
Jack Stark, Series Editor

Privileges and Immunities
David Skillen Bogen

Searches, Seizures, and Warrants
Robert M. Bloom

The Supremacy Clause
Christopher R. Drahozal

Procedural Due Process
Rhonda Wasserman

Double Jeopardy
David S. Rudstein

Freedom of the Press
Lyrissa Barnett Lidsky and R. George Wright

The Taxing Power
Erik M. Jensen

Freedom of Speech
Keith Werhan

The Religion Guarantees
Peter K. Rofes

Limits on States
James M. McGoldrick, Jr.

The Full Faith and Credit Clause
William L. Reynolds and William M. Richman

The Right to a Speedy and Public Trial
Susan N. Herman

The Power to Legislate
Richard E. Levy

Powers Reserved for the People and the States
Thomas B. McAffee

Judicial Jurisdiction

A Reference Guide to the United States Constitution

Patrick Baude

REFERENCE GUIDES TO THE
UNITED STATES CONSTITUTION, NUMBER 19
Jack Stark, *Series Editor*

PRAEGER

Westport, Connecticut
London

Library of Congress Cataloging-in-Publication Data
Baude, Patrick.
Judicial jurisdiction : a reference guide to the United States Constitution / Patrick Baude.
p. cm. — (Reference guides to the United States Constitution, ISSN 1539-8986; No. 19)
Includes bibliographical references and index.
ISBN 0-313-31204-4 (alk. paper)
1. Constitutional law—United States. 2. Judicial power—United States. 3.
United States. Constitution. I. Title. II. Series.
KF5130.B38 2007
342.7302—dc22 2006037772

British Library Cataloguing in Publication Data is available.

Library of Congress Catalog Card Number: 2006037772
ISBN-10: 0-313-31204-4
ISBN-13: 978-0-313-31204-5
ISSN: 1539-8986

First published in 2007

Praeger Publishers, 88 Post Road West, Westport, CT 06881
An imprint of Greenwood Publishing Group, Inc.
www.praeger.com

Printed in the United States of America

The paper used in this book complies with the
Permanent Paper Standard issued by the National
Information Standards Organization (Z39.48–1984).

10 9 8 7 6 5 4 3 2 1

To Ralph F. Fuchs (1899–1985), scholar, advocate,
friend, and source of inspiration to many

Contents

Series Foreword

Jack Stark

One can conceive of the United States Constitution in many ways. For example, noting the reverence in which it has been held, one can think of it as equivalent to a sacred text. Unfortunately, most of its devotees have had less knowledge and even less understanding of the document than they have had reverence for it. Sometimes it is treated as primarily a political document and on that basis has been subjected to analysis, such as Charles Beard's *An Economic Interpretation of the Constitution of the United States*. One can plausibly argue that the Constitution seems most astounding when it is seen in the light of the intellectual effort that has been associated with it. Three brief but highly intense bursts of intellectual energy produced, and established as organic law, most of the Constitution as it now exists. Two of these efforts, sustained over a long period of time, have enabled us better to understand that document.

The first burst of energy occurred at the Constitutional Convention. Although some of the delegates' business, such as the struggle between populous and nonpopulous states about their representation in Congress, was political, much of it was about fundamental issues of political theory. A few of the delegates had or later achieved international eminence for their intellects. Among them were Benjamin Franklin, Alexander Hamilton, and James Madison. Others, although less well known, had first-rate minds. That group includes George Mason and George Wythe. Many of the delegates contributed intelligently. Although the Convention's records are less than satisfactory, they indicate clearly enough that the delegates worked mightily to constitute not merely a polity but a rational polity—one that would rise to the standards envisioned by the delegates' intellectual ancestors. Their product, though brief, is amazing. William Gladstone called it "the most wonderful work ever struck off."

Despite the delegates' eminence and the Constitution's excellence as seen from our place in history, its ratification was far from certain. That state of affairs necessitated the second burst of intellectual energy associated with that document: the debate over ratification. Soon after the Convention adjourned, articles and speeches—some supporting the Constitution and some attacking it—began to proliferate. A national debate commenced, not only about the document itself, but also about the nature of the polity that ought to exist in this country. Both sides included many writers and speakers who were verbally adroit and steeped in the relevant political and philosophical literature. The result was an accumulation of material that is remarkable for both its quantity and its quality. At its apex is *The Federalist Papers*, a production of Alexander Hamilton, James Madison, and John Jay that deserves a place among the great books of Western culture.

Another burst, not as impressive as the first two but highly respectable, occurred when the Bill of Rights was proposed. Some delegates to the Constitutional Convention had vigorously asserted that such guarantees should be included in the original document. George Mason, the principal drafter of the Virginia Declaration of Rights, so held, and he walked out of the Convention when he failed to achieve his purpose. Even those who had argued that the rights in question were implicit recognized the value of adding protection of them to the Constitution. The debate was thus focused on the rights that were to be explicitly granted, not on whether any rights *ought* to be explicitly granted. Again many writers and speakers entered the fray, and again the debate was solidly grounded in theory and was conducted on a high intellectual level.

Thus, within a few years a statement of organic law and a vital coda to it had been produced. However, the meaning and effect of many of that document's provisions were far from certain; the debates on ratification of the Constitution and the Bill of Rights had demonstrated that. In addition, the document existed in a vacuum, because statutes and actions had not been assessed by its standards. The attempt to resolve these problems began after Chief Justice John Marshall, in Marbury v. Madison, asserted the right of the U.S. Supreme Court to interpret and apply the Constitution. Judicial interpretation and application of the Constitution, beginning with the first constitutional case and persisting until the most recent, is one of the sustained exertions of intellectual energy associated with the Constitution. The framers would be surprised by some of the results of those activities. References in the document to "due process," which seems to refer only to procedures, have been held also to have a substantive dimension. A right to privacy has been found lurking among the penumbras of various parts of the text. A requirement that states grant the same "privileges and immunities" to citizens of other states that they granted to their own citizens, which seemed to guarantee important rights, was held not to be particularly important. The corpus of judicial interpretations of the Constitution is now as voluminous as that document is terse.

As the judicial interpretations multiplied, another layer—interpretations of interpretations—appeared, and also multiplied. This layer, the other sustained intellectual effort associated with the Constitution, consists of articles, most of them published in law reviews, and books on the Constitution. This material varies in quality and significance. Some of these works of scholarship result from meticulous examination and incisive thought. Others repeat earlier work, or apply a fine-tooth comb to matters that are too minute even for such a comb. Somewhere in that welter of tertiary material is the answer to almost every question that one could ask about constitutional law. The problem is finding the answer that one wants. The difficulty of locating useful guidance is exacerbated by the bifurcation of most constitutional scholarship into two kinds. In "Two Styles of Social Science Research," C. Wright Mills delineates macroscopic and molecular research. The former deals with huge issues, the latter with tiny issues. Virtually all of the scholarship on the Constitution is of one of those two types. Little of it is macroscopic, but that category does include some first-rate syntheses such as Jack Rakove's *Original Meanings.* Most constitutional scholarship is molecular, and, again, some fine work is included in that category.

In his essay, Mills bemoans the inability of social scientists to combine the two kinds of research that he describes to create a third category that will be more generally useful. This series of books is an attempt to do for constitutional law the intellectual work that Mills proposed for social science. The author of each book has dealt carefully and at reasonable length with a topic that lies in the middle range of generality. Upon completion, this series will consist of thirty-seven books, each on a constitutional law topic. Some of the books, such as the book on freedom of the press, explicate one portion of the Constitution's text. Others, such as the volume on federalism, treat a topic that has several anchors in the Constitution. The books on constitutional history and constitutional interpretation range over the entire document, but each does so from one perspective. Except for a very few of the books, for which special circumstances dictate minor changes in format, each book includes the same components: a brief history of the topic, a lengthy and sophisticated analysis of the current state of the law on that topic, a bibliographical essay that organizes and evaluates scholarly material in order to facilitate further research, a table of cases, and an index. The books are intellectually rigorous—in fact, authorities have written them—but, due to their clarity and to brief definitions of terms that are unfamiliar to laypersons, each is comprehensible and useful to a wide audience, one that ranges from other experts on the book's subject to intelligent nonlawyers.

In short, this series provides an extremely valuable service to the legal community and to others who are interested in constitutional law, as every citizen should be. Each book is a map of part of the U.S. Constitution. Together they map all of that document's territory that is worth mapping. When this series is complete, each book will be a third kind of scholarly work that combines the macroscopic and the molecular. Together they will explicate all of the important constitutional topics. Anyone who wants assistance in understanding either a topic in constitutional law or the Constitution as a whole can easily find it in these books.

Acknowledgments

I am grateful to Darren A. Craig, Richard B. Sorrell, Dione C. Greene, and Jonathan B. Warner. All four individuals provided research assistance while students at Indiana University.

I am grateful to Lauren Robel and John Applegate for their encouragement and support.

And I am grateful to Marjorie A. Young and Stacey Harris for facing down the gremlins of word processing.

Introduction

This work is devoted to Article III, section 2, of the U.S. Constitution. Section 1, which is not my subject, creates the Supreme Court and defines the independence of the judicial branch. This is the glamorous part. Section 2 deals with the rather more ordinary question of what actual work these courts will have to do. I believe that the practical arrangements of section 2 have much to do with the success of the judicial branch in the constitutional system. In most of the world's democracies, the power of judicial review is vested in a specialized court of some sort, which does not muddy its hands with everyday legal work. The strength of the American courts is the institutional arrangement that makes all the nation's courts carry the same burdens—that is, the great business of telling the truth to power in moments of crisis along with determining who is at fault when a train injures a pedestrian. This common cause helps to make us believe that our constitution is real law, not just a shiny set of quasi-legal aspirations. The foundation of the rule of law is deciding cases day in and day out, not the making of occasional eloquent statements of political theory.

I do not attempt to survey the intricate details of jurisdiction, many of which are legislative creations rather than constitutional matters. My aim is to trace the organizing ideas of federal judicial jurisdiction and provide a sense of what has been controversial. My plan is to show how our judicial system is a cooperative project between Congress and the courts. My hope is that the next time the reader runs across section 2, she or he will not rush through it looking for the big ideas but instead will linger on the details.

Article III, Section 2

The judicial Power shall extend to all Cases, in Law and Equity, arising under this Constitution, the Laws of the United States, and Treaties made, or which shall be made, under their Authority;—to all Cases affecting Ambassadors, other public Ministers and Consuls;—to all Cases of admiralty and maritime Jurisdiction;—to

Controversies to which the United States shall be a Party;—to Controversies between two or more States;—between a State and Citizens of another State—between Citizens of the same State claiming Lands under Grants of different States, and between a State, or the Citizens thereof, and foreign States, Citizens or Subjects.

In all Cases affecting Ambassadors, other public Ministers and Consuls, and those in which a State shall be Party, the supreme Court shall have original Jurisdiction. In all the other Cases before mentioned, the supreme Court shall have appellate Jurisdiction, both as to Law and Fact, with such Exceptions, and under such Regulations as the Congress shall make.

The Trial of all Crimes, except in Cases of Impeachment, shall be by Jury; and such Trial shall be held in the State where the said Crimes shall have been committed; but when not committed within any State, the Trial shall be at such Place or Places as the Congress may by Law have directed.

Part I

A History of the Federal Court System

THE COLONIAL SYSTEM

Before the Revolution, individual colonies had separate court systems that varied considerably from one colony to the next. By and large, these systems were not particularly respected: they were, as one observer noted, "more pompous than learned."[1] The idea of separation of powers was not well developed, and the idea of an independent judiciary was not part of the intellectual furniture of the colonial mind. Decisions of the local courts were typically appealed either to the governor or the legislature, and then to London, to the Privy Council. The Privy Council combined the judicial authority to review all judgments by colonial courts with the legislative power to overturn colonial statutes on grounds, essentially, of public policy.[2] Historians mostly agree that these combined functions of legislative veto and judicial review were part of the background of the establishment of judicial review in the U.S. Supreme Court.[3] At the same time, however, the lack of a neutral judicial authority was one of the complaints against the colonial system. As the Declaration of Independence put it, "He has obstructed the Administration of Justice, by refusing his Assent to Laws for establishing Judiciary powers. He has made Judges dependent on his Will alone, for the tenure of their offices, and the amount and payment of their salaries."

Whatever the shortcomings of the colonial judicial system, it seemed to perform well in two essential functions that were later incorporated into the Articles of Confederation and then into the language of the Constitution. Most important, the Privy Council had the power to settle border disputes among the colonies, a power it exercised on nine separate occasions. Also, courts of admiralty in the colonies were necessary to resolve disputes concerning navigation, seizures, and, to some extent, the laws regulating maritime trade. These courts in the colonies were at first reviewed by the High Court of Admiralty in London, a respected court of some independence, rather than the more political Privy Council. At the end of the colonial period, admiralty courts were more involved in the unpopular business of trade regulation, and, ultimately, appellate jurisdiction over them was moved to Privy Council. It seems likely that the admiralty courts would have declined in public respect if the Revolution had not interrupted this decline. Even during the revolutionary war itself, the colonists saw the need to create admiralty courts. One key function of admiralty is to award prize money to ships' crews for the capture of enemy shipping, and the individual states gave their own courts the power to hear such cases, with appeal to a court of appeals in Cases of Capture, sanctioned by the Continental Congress and supported by General Washington. As the war continued, however, the state admiralty courts displayed many shortcomings, especially in-state bias by allowing local privateers to seize ships of neutral nations, in doing so, rejecting congressional oversight and risking the loss of support from the international community.[4]

THE ARTICLES OF CONFEDERATION

The Articles of Confederation, ratified in 1781, did not establish anything like a national court system.[5] This fact is hardly surprising, because the Articles likewise did not establish a national government with legislative or executive power to act directly on citizens. But the lessons of the immediate past were not forgotten. Article IX gave Congress the power of "appointing courts for the trial of piracies and felonies committed on the high seas and establishing courts for receiving and determining finally appeals in all cases of captures." In a reprise of one power exercised by the Privy Council, Article IX also provided an awkward system for constituting an ad hoc body of "commissioners or judges" to resolve boundary disputes among the states. However awkward, this process resolved three disputes peacefully. In at least one situation, the absence of a national court did threaten the Confederation. The Peace Treaty with Great Britain permitted British subjects to recover property and enforce contractual debts. When individual states ignored these guarantees, as they sometimes did, Britain used the treaty violation to justify its refusal to vacate western forts called for under the same treaty, which in turn enabled some tribes to retain lands sought by the states. Perhaps the most important effect of the Confederation's court system was that it made judges politically respectable by the end of the period. The situation had changed enough from the condemnation of judges in the Declaration of Independence to the time of the Constitutional Convention that six of the thirty-nine men who signed the Constitution in Philadelphia had become judges.[6]

THE CONSTITUTIONAL CONVENTION

From today's political perspective, the surprising thing about the drafting of Article III, section 2, which defines the powers of the judicial branch, is how little debate and controversy were involved. Today, we think of the judicial power as the essence of our constitutional democracy. This was not, however, the way the founders saw the matter. For them, the hard questions were defining the power of the national government versus that of the states as well as the power of the states against each other. Given these major conflicts, the creation of a judiciary was more than a detail but certainly not one of the big ideas at the time.

Article III begins by providing how the federal court system should be structured. The provisions in section 1 shaped the concepts in section 2, which were not deeply discussed or debated in isolation. That there should be a Supreme Court was taken for granted. The power of the Court to enforce constitutional limits in at least some cases was little discussed but widely assumed. Whether there should be other federal courts was left to be decided by Congress over the years to come. The most distinctive feature of our constitutional courts is the fact that even the lowest federal courts have the power, in routine cases, to strike down acts of Congress or issue judgments setting aside presidential orders. Today, almost every nation has a high court with the power to apply its national constitution to the government. The United States, however, is almost alone in vesting that power in every level of the judicial system—and it is, indeed, that unique vesting of an ultimate power that is the foundation of our national belief, one might almost say national "faith," that the rule of law and the supremacy of the Constitution are the same thing.

The Philadelphia Convention began its substantive discussion by adopting the plan put forth by Edmund Randolph.[7] Randolph was a Virginia lawyer who favored the interests of the big states. His plan first called for the creation of "one *or more* supreme tribunals." The notion of more than one federal "supreme" court seems odd now but drew upon English practice of separate courts for the different systems of law, equity, and admiralty. There was little discussion in detail of the concept of multiple supreme courts, and the general principle of a national supreme court was accepted without dissent. The then-recent problems with the absence of such a tribunal under the Articles of Confederation probably sealed the deal.

Second, Randolph's plan called for the creation of a system of lower federal courts. The delegates initially approved this proposal without debate or dissent. The next day, however, South Carolina's John Rutledge moved to reconsider the creation of lower federal courts. This time there was a sharp debate, with James Madison vigorously defending the Randolph plan, describing Rutledge's proposal as the "mere trunk of a body without arms or legs to act or move." In a closely divided and inconclusive vote (five states for, four against, two undecided), the delegates adopted Rutledge's plan to eliminate the lower federal courts.[8] But Madison then proposed a compromise: to give Congress the discretion to create, or not, tribunals inferior to the Supreme Court. This compromise quickly carried the day and was not seriously challenged thereafter.

Third, Randolph's plan called for the appointment of judges by the legislature. This would have given large states significant power in the resulting choices. This proposal led to a pointed debate between the small states, which typically favored Senate appointment of judges, and the large states, which came to support presidential appointment. This issue was resolved late in the convention and only as part of a general compromise on the appointment power. The compromise seems pretty obvious: the president nominates and the Senate decides. In the current political context, there is much controversy regarding how, exactly, the Senate and the president should define their share of this dual power and its effect on the ideology of the judges. The delegates in Philadelphia appear not to have anticipated that judicial nominations would become ideological and were concerned mainly with checking "a spirit of favoritism."[9] The delegates on all sides of the appointment question generally accepted the principle that judges would hold office during good behavior and that their compensation could not be diminished. There was some discussion of prohibiting salary increases as well, which had in fact been prohibited by the earliest proposals—outlawing the carrot as well as the stick. In the end, however, mainly in recognition of the possibility of inflation, the final language allowed increases but not decreases. At one point, later in the convention, Delaware's John Dickinson proposed that judges could be removed by the president on application from the legislature, but that motion failed overwhelmingly, with support only from Connecticut.

Fourth, Randolph's plan specified the jurisdiction of the federal courts, but only in the broadest terms. All agreed that the exact provisions should be worked out by the Committee of Detail. Randolph's general language, which spoke of "all cases of national revenue, impeachment of national officers, and questions which involve the national peace or harmony" was unanimously modified to read "all cases arising under the Nat'l laws: And to such other questions as may involve the Nat'l peace & harmony."[10] The actual language of Article III, section 2, is the product of the Committee of Detail (with minor changes in the Committee of Style). There are only sparse records of that Committee's deliberation and, hence, little illumination of why particular words were chosen.

What became section 2 contains seven clauses, separated from each other by semicolons and dashes, conferring jurisdiction on the federal court system as a whole. As the system developed, two of those clauses have come to define the central role of the court system. First, the introductory clause provides that "The judicial Power shall extend to all Cases, in Law and Equity, arising under this Constitution, the Laws of the United States, and Treaties made, or which shall be made, under their Authority." Known today as "federal question" jurisdiction, this is the heart of what we now think federal courts exist to do. Most of the historical controversies over the years have involved this heading of jurisdiction. The second defining clause deals with what is usually called "diversity" jurisdiction, with controversies "between Citizens of different States." The purpose of this clause was not explained at the convention and is generally assumed to be aimed at preventing locally biased adjudication, a purpose that seems to many fairly irrelevant in these global times, as racial, ethnic, class, and cultural antagonisms overwhelm in-state favoritism. The remaining clauses in section 2 confer judicial jurisdiction over suits to which the United States or a state is party, admiralty cases, and controversies affecting diplomats, between states, involving foreign states and citizens, and between citizens claiming land by deeds from different states. These remaining clauses all seem targeted at easy-to-see abuses resulting from the absence of national courts under the Articles of Confederation. It is mainly the federal question and diversity clauses that broke new ground, although there was little discussion of their exact meaning. The analysis section of this volume is largely devoted to exploring how those two ideas have evolved.

Had the delegates adopted a plan requiring the creation of lower federal courts there would have been little need to apportion jurisdiction between the Supreme Court and lower courts. It would have been enough, and obvious, simply to treat the Supreme Court as having appellate jurisdiction to be defined by Congress as it defined lower courts. Given the compromise that actually was adopted, however, allowing for the possibility that there might be no other federal courts, it became important to specify whether the Supreme Court also had original jurisdiction. Otherwise, there could be no guarantee that any cases at all would be tried initially in a federal court. When the Committee of Detail was working on this question, the larger plan still contemplated that cases of impeachment would be tried in the courts, rather than in the Senate as ultimately settled. So an early committee draft gave the Supreme Court original jurisdiction in impeachment and "such other cases as the legislature might prescribe." The final draft from the Committee added cases affecting diplomats (ambassadors, public ministers, and consuls), and, once this proposal was back before the convention for final approval, the convention deleted the phrase giving Congress the power to add to the Court's original jurisdiction[11]—a deletion that was soon to set the stage for the great case of Marbury v. Madison.

Throughout the Committee's deliberations, it was agreed, of course, that the remainder of the Supreme Court's jurisdiction would be appellate. Perhaps the obviousness of this basic point explains the casualness with which two key phrases were added to the final language as it appears in Article III: "the supreme Court shall have appellate Jurisdiction, both as to Law *and Fact*, with such *Exceptions*, and under such Regulations as the Congress shall make" (emphasis added).[12] The exact scope of this authority of Congress to make "exceptions" to the Supreme Court's jurisdiction on appeal has today become one of the great unanswered questions of separation of powers. The addition of the word "fact" raised serious questions about the scope of trial by jury when the Constitution was submitted to the states for ratification. The final section of Article III provided in general terms for jury trial in criminal cases, but this language, too, was to become a crucial issue in the ratification process.

RATIFICATION DEBATES IN THE STATE CONVENTIONS

There may have been little fuss over Article III at the Constitutional Convention in Philadelphia, but the state ratifying conventions were harder to satisfy. The states were concerned most of all with the question of trial by jury. The founding generation, no doubt, deeply respected the role of the jury. The Declaration of Independence itself had listed as a primary grievance against the English king that he had deprived them "of the Benefits of Trial by Jury." Three separate items in Article III fueled these concerns: (1) the language giving the Supreme Court appellate jurisdiction "as to . . . Fact"; (2) the potential argument that explicit protection of the right to trial by jury in criminal cases had, by implication, negated the right in civil cases, which was not otherwise mentioned; and (3) the wording of the criminal jury right itself, which provided only for trial in the state where the crime was committed, leaving open the possibility of trying defendants hundreds of miles away from the crime scene and in front of total strangers.[13]

The pro-Constitution forces offered two basic replies to these concerns. The first was that Congress would take care of these details. If Congress did decide to accept the opportunity offered by Article III to set up lower federal courts, it would without doubt arrange for civil juries. Similarly, if Congress set up lower courts for criminal charges, it could be trusted to ensure that the place of trial was appropriate. More generally, the Constitution's defenders argued, the question of civil jury trial was by its nature too detailed, too contingent, and too complex to be set by a simple provision. At the time, in English practice, there were jury trials in common-law courts but not in courts of equity or admiralty. Figuring out where a particular dispute would be tried was often a perplexing problem and to some extent subject to the discretion inherent in equity courts. Adding considerably to the problem in real-world terms, the individual states at the time varied in their own practices of law and equity.[14] This complexity would, in turn, carry over to the Supreme Court's appellate jurisdiction. In equity and admiralty cases, English courts on appeal typically did, or at least could, decide factual issues because there had not been a jury at the trial level. Also important is the fact that our modern sense of appellate and trial courts was not a fact of life in 1789: "Most states had a corps of judges who sometimes went singly into the field to try cases, and who at other times assembled together in the capital to try cases and consider 'appeals.'"[15] Our modern American conception of sharply defined differences between appeals and trials is, perhaps ironically, derived from efforts beginning with the First Congress to allay some of the anti-Federalist concerns expressed during the ratification process.

Independent of the jury issue, convention delegates resented the diversity (between citizens of different states) and alienage jurisdictions as unneeded and even insulting to the dignity of state courts. The most direct reply to the diversity question was offered at some length in Hamilton's 80th Federalist paper, which described it as "essential to the peace of the union," contrasting the "horrid picture of the dissentions and private wars which distracted and desolated Germany." To avoid "evasion and subterfuge," he argued, it was necessary to assign such controversies to tribunals with "no local attachments."[16] Both the jury and diversity objections were temporarily set aside so that ratification could allow the new government to be formed. It was, however, clearly understood that these questions would be high on the agenda of the newly elected Congress, and so they were.

THE FIRST CONGRESS

The right to trial by jury was not the only issue of individual rights to arise at the state ratifying conventions. Dealing with the entire set of issues was one item for the first session of the new Congress. As a collective solution, Congress proposed the constitutional amendments that are now known as the Bill of Rights. Among these amendments, the Sixth Amendment adds greater specificity to the jury in criminal cases, and the Seventh Amendment adds a new provision guaranteeing trial by jury in civil cases. Those amendments have superseded any possible effects from Article III (the interested reader should turn to the separate volumes on each amendment in this series).

A larger part of the first Congress's work, however, was the task of filling in the blanks left by the compromises in Article III. Akhil Amar suggests that a key to understanding the entire Constitution is this recognition of how incomplete Article III was.[17] Article I, which establishes the legislature, is long and excruciatingly detailed. Article II, fixing the executive power, is less than half the length of Article I, and Article III, in turn, less than half the length of Article II. Both the length and placement reflect the idea that the substantive provisions that came first, and closest to the "We the People" who begin the preamble, create an elected legislature that has the basic responsibility for completing the details as the document continues.

The Judiciary Act of 1789, in effect, completed the structure whose foundation was laid in Article III. First, Congress did in fact exercise the option to create a system of lower federal courts, which have been with the nation ever since, although the details have varied over the years. This decision was the only one "on which significant debate was reported."[18] These courts were given jurisdiction in admiralty cases and in diversity and alienage cases where more than $500 was in controversy (an amount that has increased over the years, reaching $75,000 at present).[19] Notably lacking from the jurisdiction of the trial courts was any general provision for hearing cases involving federal legal or constitutional cases. Federal courts could try criminal and statutory penalty cases and suits by aliens for certain violations of international law,[20] but they could not otherwise hear a case simply because it was one "arising under this Constitution, the Laws of the United States . . ." as specified in Article III. That general power over federal questions was not vested until the Judiciary Act of 1875,[21] consolidating the constitutional transformation wrought by the Civil War. Even before 1875, various particular statutes adopted after 1789 sometimes gave jurisdiction to enforce one or another limited federal statute—for example, the banking statute involved in Osborn v. Bank of the United States, discussed later in part I. The important thing about this picture of jurisdiction is how different it looks from the modern federal courts, which have become the main forum for the assertion of federal rights.

Second, the 1789 Act conferred a general appellate jurisdiction on the Supreme Court, limited however in two respects: (1) the Supreme Court could hear appeals within the federal system but not in criminal cases; and (2) the Court could only hear appeals from state courts in cases in which an alleged federal right had been denied by the state courts. There was, for example, no power to hear an appeal in a diversity case and no power to hear a complaint by the losing party when the state court was alleged to have erred in extending too far a claimed federal right. Like the federal question jurisdiction of the trial courts, the limited scope of Supreme Court power to review state courts was significantly expanded by the Judiciary Act of 1875. Probably the most famous section of the 1789 Act, however, was to become section 13. The second paragraph of Article III, section 2, had conferred upon the Supreme Court a narrow category of original jurisdiction. In addition to repeating this language, the 1789 Act provided in section 13 that federal courts could issue writs of mandamus. The possible argument that section 13 would allow anyone seeking such a writ to sue directly in the Supreme Court gave rise to the monumental case of Marbury v. Madison.

Marbury v. Madison and the Judicial Power

In a colorful political tale, President John Adams nominated William Marbury to be a justice of the peace for the county of Washington in the District of Columbia. The appointment was part of a last-minute plan to stack the judicial branch with loyal Federalists, preventing the newly elected president, Thomas Jefferson, from placing his own sympathizers on the bench. The Senate confirmed Marbury's nomination, President Adams signed his commission, the seal of the United States was affixed, and the commission disappeared from the historical record. Marbury brought an action in the Supreme Court seeking a writ of mandamus under the somewhat ambiguous authorization of section 13 of the 1789 Act. Such a writ would have ordered the secretary of state, James Madison, to produce the undelivered commission, defying a contrary instruction from President Jefferson.

In 1801, the Court found that the case involved three issues. The first issue examined whether Marbury had a right to his commission. This discussion seems impenetrable to the modern mind—today, sealed documents lack the gripping power they had over eighteenth-century lawyers. The second issue was, if Marbury's right had been violated, did the laws of the United States provide him with a remedy? After a remarkably extended discussion, the answer is "of course, even Thomas Jefferson isn't allowed to steal things that belong to others." The third issue was whether the proper remedy was a writ of mandamus issued by the Supreme Court. The Court held that, while a writ of mandamus was the proper remedy, the Supreme Court did not have jurisdiction to issue it.

The question of whether the Supreme Court had jurisdiction to issue a writ of mandamus required the Court to consider whether a provision of the Judiciary Act of 1789 was consistent with Article III of the Constitution. The Judiciary Act of 1789 authorized the Supreme Court "to issue writs of mandamus, in cases warranted by the principles and usages of law, to any courts appointed, or persons holding office under the authority of the United States." The Court found that issuing a writ of mandamus is an exercise of original, rather than appellate, jurisdiction. Hence, the Court confronted the conflict between the Judiciary Act and the Constitution. Article III of the Constitution provides that "the supreme Court shall have original Jurisdiction" over "all Cases affecting Ambassadors, other public Ministers and Consuls, and those in which a State shall be Party. In all the other Cases ... the supreme Court shall have appellate Jurisdiction." Thus, the Judiciary Act appears to confer original jurisdiction on the Supreme Court where the Constitution does not, at least in explicit terms. Article III does not explicitly say that the cases listed in the original jurisdiction language are the only ones that could be placed in that category. In the same vein, section 13 of the Judiciary Act simply authorizes the Supreme Court to issue a writ of mandamus where appropriate, and it does not, in its terms, say that the Court will have jurisdiction any time anybody in the world wants such a writ. It is hard to escape the conclusion that Chief Justice Marshall was looking for a conflict because he wanted one to write about.

Marshall's opinion for the Court went on to hold that where an act of Congress conflicts with the Constitution, the act of Congress is void. The Court noted that the Constitution described certain limits to the powers of each branch of government. Therefore, the Court reasoned, Congress cannot transcend those limits by legislative act or else the limits described in the Constitution are meaningless. Furthermore, where the courts must decide a case in which the act of Congress would lead to one conclusion, and the Constitution a different conclusion, courts should follow the Constitution and not the statute. Because it is the "province" of the judiciary to say what the law is, when courts are confronted with conflicting laws, they must decide which law applies. Courts would have to say the statute is unconstitutional or that the Constitution is unstatutory. The latter phrase is, at the least, hard to conceptualize.

The Court offered three other arguments for the conclusion that in situations in which acts of Congress conflict with the Constitution, courts must follow the Constitution. First, the Court stated that the Framers intended the Constitution to provide rules for courts as well as other branches of government. For example, in Article III, the article establishing the judiciary, the Constitution provides that a court may not convict a person of treason "unless on the testimony of two witnesses to the same overt act, or on confession in open court." Second, judges must take an oath to support the Constitution. If judges cannot decide cases in conformity with the Constitution, then they must violate their oath of office. Third, the Supremacy Clause in Article VI states that only the laws made *in pursuance* of the Constitution shall be the supreme law of the land. These arguments surely do illustrate that the Constitution is supreme over a statute, but they hardly establish that the Court's interpretation of an ambiguous clause in the Constitution is the binding one. A significant number of those who adopted the Judiciary Act were themselves delegates to the Philadelphia Convention, notably including Oliver Ellsworth, the Connecticut senator who was the principal draftsman of the Judiciary Act and preceded Marshall as Chief Justice. Nor is it clear why the oath taken by a federal judge outweighs the oath required of senators and representatives by Article VI, section 3.

The case has enduring importance because of its establishment of the power in the federal courts to set aside statutes violating the judicial interpretation of the Constitution. Although the point has been much discussed by scholars and critics over the years, this basic proposition has been accepted without controversy—and the same seems to be true of the Framers in Philadelphia, who assumed, without express declarations to that effect, that the judicial function included the power to set aside statutes, if necessary. The irony here is that the case should probably be better remembered for its absolutely unnecessary interpretation that section 13 of the Judiciary Act actually purported to give the Supreme Court jurisdiction rather than allowing it to issue the writ of mandamus in cases in which it had otherwise been given jurisdiction.

Defining "Citizens of Different States": Strawbridge v. Curtiss

Strawbridge and others, some of whom were citizens of Massachusetts, brought a suit against Curtiss, a citizen of Vermont, and other citizens of

Massachusetts, in a federal trial court located in Massachusetts. The Supreme Court held in 1806 that federal courts did not have diversity jurisdiction in the case. The Judiciary Act of 1789 conferred federal jurisdiction when "an alien is a party, or the suit is between a citizen of the State where the suit is brought and a citizen of another State." Read logically, the federal courts would seem to have jurisdiction because this was, among other things, a suit between a citizen of Massachusetts, where it was brought, and a citizen of Vermont, which is another state. Read functionally, there seems to be no reason to hear the case in a federal court. If a Massachusetts state court hears the case, it will have to rule against one of its own citizens on one side and in favor of one of its own on the other side. This situation is sometimes called "partial diversity" to distinguish it from the case of "complete diversity" (e.g., all Vermonters on one side and all Massachusetts residents on the other). If there were complete diversity, then the Vermonters might legitimately fear discrimination in a Massachusetts court. There are still, however, cases of partial diversity in which discrimination might be a serious risk. The *Strawbridge* case itself, for example, might have been brought in Vermont instead of Massachusetts. In that situation, a Vermont state court could rule for Curtiss, the local favorite, and thus find against a group of people who were entirely from out of state. Or if, as was not the case in *Strawbridge*, the liability were several rather than joint, the Massachusetts court in *Strawbridge* could have rendered a judgment against Curtiss, the Vermonter, alone. These doubts about the case's rationale persisted for 150 years, until the Supreme Court ultimately decided that *Strawbridge* was only an interpretation that the Judiciary Act required complete diversity: the Constitution itself could be satisfied by partial diversity if Congress said so, as it increasingly has done in complex multiparty multistate litigation.[22]

The 1806 decision remains, however, as a basic statement that the purpose of diversity jurisdiction is to prevent local prejudice from operating against out-of-state parties. Such fears seem almost quaint in contemporary American life. Prejudice is a real fact today—racial, religious, sexual, lifestyle, ethnic, obesity, political, and so on. But the thought that Vermonters and residents of Massachusetts would see each other as enemies rather than New Englanders aligned together against the world is hard to accept as an systematically important concern. This changed worldview about localism may help to explain why diversity jurisdiction barely figures in the popular view of what is important about federal courts.

Martin v. Hunter's Lessee and Appellate Jurisdiction over State Courts

Despite the clarity of Article III's language, the growing friction of federalism led some state courts to believe that the Supreme Court of the United

States could not exercise jurisdiction over them. The sentiments and ideology involved, about the nature of sovereignty itself, were similar to those underlying the possibility of secession. Martin's case in 1816 became the vehicle for demonstrating the clarity of Article III. The Court's decision was written by Justice Story, Chief Justice Marshall having recused himself because the underlying dispute concerned land transactions in which his brother was a substantial investor.

The plaintiff brought an action of ejectment in Virginia state court. The plaintiff held title to land under a patent granted by Virginia in 1789. Virginia claimed title by escheat or forfeiture. The defendant claimed title as the devisee of Lord Fairfax. The defendant further claimed that his title was protected by the peace treaty of 1783 between the United States and Great Britain. The state trial court at Winchester, Virginia, entered judgment for the defendant, which was reversed by the highest state court. The defendant then appealed to the U.S. Supreme Court, which reversed in turn. After the case was then remanded to the Virginia Court of Appeals, that state court refused to comply with the mandate of the Supreme Court. The Virginia court concluded that the federal government could not directly compel any state agency to act. This argument seems to have been based on a sense of protocol more than logic, history, or constitutional language. Nonetheless, the Virginia court found section 25 of the Judiciary Act unconstitutional and thus rejected the mandate. Had the opinion been Marshall's to write, one can easily imagine the organ tones in which he would have talked about parts and wholes, about nations and covenants, about fate and historical necessity. Story, however, was the sort of judge who cared more for careful and sober details.

The Court in Story's measured logic held that it could review the Virginia court's decision. The Court noted that Article III gives it appellate jurisdiction over all the subjects specified in Article III, except those over which it has original jurisdiction. According to the terms of Article III, then, it is the subject of the case—and not the court in which the case originates—that gives the Supreme Court jurisdiction. The Court also reasoned that if it could not review the decisions of state courts, then state courts could not consider cases involving the Constitution, federal laws, or treaties. The Constitution grants the Supreme Court jurisdiction over cases involving, among other things, the Constitution, federal laws, and treaties. If a case that was originally heard in state court cannot be reviewed in the Supreme Court, then it must follow that state courts cannot hear cases involving federal questions. The Supremacy Clause, however, shows that the Framers of the Constitution intended that state courts could hear cases involving federal questions. The Supremacy Clause provides that "the judges in every state shall be bound [by the Constitution, federal laws, and treaties.]" Because state courts can hear cases involving federal questions, it follows that the appellate power of the United States must extend to some cases that originate in state courts.

The Court advanced several other arguments for extending the appellate power of the Supreme Court to cases originally heard in state court. First, the Court noted that if a state executive or state legislature acts contrary to the Constitution, the Supreme Court can declare those acts to be void. There is no reason why the Supreme Court should have less power over state courts than over other branches of state government.

Second, the Court argued that unless it has the final word on the interpretation of the Constitution, federal statutes, and treaties, those bodies of law will be subject to widely varying interpretations in the various states. Finally, the Court argued that its appellate jurisdiction is founded on the same authority as its removal jurisdiction. According to the Court, Congress can authorize the removal of certain cases from state to federal court because those cases lie within the appellate power of federal courts. In removal, however, the appellate power is exercised before, rather than after, judgment. Thus, if Congress may authorize removal of certain cases from state to federal court, then Congress may also authorize federal courts to review certain state court decisions.

After concluding that its appellate power extended to the Virginia case, the Court asserted that it had the power not only to consider the correctness of the interpretation the Virginia court gave to the treaty, but also to consider the validity of the title claimed under the treaty. The Court has this authority, it argued, because it is impossible to decide whether the treaty protects the title without determining whether the title is valid.

This case also contains Justice Story's discussion of whether Congress has the discretion to confer on federal courts less than the full jurisdiction granted by the Constitution. Story argues that because Article III provides that "[t]he judicial power of the United States *shall* be vested in one supreme court, and in such inferior courts as the Congress may from time to time ordain and establish," Congress is required to vest federal courts with the whole judicial power of the United States, as that power is defined in the Constitution. In Story's view, the word "shall" made conferring jurisdiction on courts mandatory. Furthermore, because the Supreme Court can exercise original jurisdiction in only a limited class of federal cases, it follows that Congress is obliged to establish some lower federal courts. In the analysis section of this volume, we shall consider the effect of Story's position on the general power of Congress to control federal courts by restrictions on their jurisdiction.

Osborn v. Bank of the United States: The Beginning of Federal Questions in Federal Trial Courts

Recall that the 1789 Judiciary Act gave federal trial courts the general jurisdiction to hear all cases arising under the Constitution and laws of the United States. The *Osborn* case, in 1824, however, involved a particular statute chartering the Bank of the United States and conferring relevant jurisdiction on the federal courts.

The Bank of the United States was established by an act of Congress that provided as part of the Bank's articles of incorporation that it shall be "made able and capable in law ... to sue and be sued, plead and be impleaded, answer and be answered, defend and be defended, in all State Courts having competent jurisdiction, and in any Circuit Court of the United States."

In a mood of hostility toward the national banking project and in defense of soft currency, the Ohio state legislature provided by statute for a tax against all banks that transacted business in Ohio without being authorized by statute to do so. The Bank of the United States then filed suit in the federal circuit court for Ohio seeking an injunction to prevent Ralph Osborn, the Auditor of the State of Ohio, from collecting the tax. The court issued the injunction, but one of Osborn's employees, J. L. Harper, collected the tax anyway. The court ordered the return of the money seized from the Bank. Osborn and Harper then appealed. On appeal, Osborn and Harper presented the issue whether the Bank had the right to sue in federal court. They argued that the Bank did not have that power in this case because the resolution of the case depended not on any federal law but on "general principles" of law.

The Supreme Court held that the Bank did have the right to sue in federal court. The Court reasoned that the Bank was able to file suit only because it was authorized to do so by an act of Congress; cases in which the Bank is a party *necessarily* involve the laws of the United States. The Court also held that if one element of the case gave a federal court jurisdiction over the case, the federal court could decide all issues involved in the case. The Court stated:

> If it be a sufficient foundation for jurisdiction, that the title or right set up by the party, may be defeated by one construction of the constitution or law of the United States, and sustained by the opposite construction, provided the facts necessary to support the action be made out, then all the other questions must be decided as incidental to this, which gives that jurisdiction.[23]

On the next page of the opinion just quoted, the Court provided a slightly different formulation of this rule:

> [W]hen a question to which the judicial power of the Union is extended by the constitution, forms an ingredient of the original cause, it is in the power of Congress to give the Circuit Courts jurisdiction of that cause, although other questions of fact or of law may be involved in it.[24]

In support of this rule, the Court pointed out that almost all cases depend, in part, on factors other than the Constitution, federal laws, or treaties. If those nonfederal legal and factual questions could not be decided by a federal court, then federal courts would almost never be able to decide an entire case.

The Court found support for the Bank's right to sue in federal court by drawing an analogy with other areas of federal law. For example, the postmaster general has the right to sue in federal court because an act of Congress gives him or her that right. In patent law, a litigant may sue in federal court even if the cause of action has nothing to do with the validity of the patent, but rather pertains to factual questions that do not depend on federal law.

The appellant in this case argued against permitting the Bank to sue in federal court by drawing an analogy between the Bank and naturalized citizens. The rights of a naturalized citizen under the laws of the United States depend on an act of Congress, just as the rights of the Bank depend on an act of Congress. The act of Congress conferring citizenship on an alien, however, does not give the naturalized citizen the right to sue in federal court. The Court did not find the appellants' analogy persuasive because the act of Congress conferring citizenship does not provide the naturalized citizens with any rights other than those that follow from being a citizen. In contrast, the act incorporating the Bank conferred on the Bank the right to sue in federal court.

Justice Johnson dissented. He argued that federal courts did not have jurisdiction over the case because no issues of federal law were involved in the case. Because the dispute between the Bank and the agents of Ohio involved questions of the state law of trespass, the outcome of the case did not depend in any way on federal law. The fact that the Bank was created by an act of Congress did not change the underlying factual or legal questions in the case.

This case also involved an Eleventh Amendment question. The agents of Ohio argued that the Eleventh Amendment gave them immunity from being sued in federal court. The Court disagreed, stating that:

> [I]n all cases where jurisdiction depends on the party, it is the party named in the record. Consequently, the 11th amendment, which restrains the jurisdiction granted by the constitution over suits against States, is, of necessity, limited to those suits in which a State is a party on the record.[25]

The subsequent history of the Eleventh Amendment, one of the cornerstones of our federalism, is the subject of another volume of this series.

The *Osborn* case articulated the scope of power over federal questions in the broadest terms conceivable. Needless to say, it was a Marshall opinion and showed his broad brush rather than the cautious lawyering Justice Story might have provided. Since 1875, most practical litigation has turned on the statutory grant of "arising under" rather than the potential power under Article III. When necessary, however, the sweep of Osborn's holding may remain available as a justification should Congress decide to expand further the power of federal courts.

Swift v. Tyson and the Federal Common Law

Article III allows Congress to confer jurisdiction on federal courts for suits between citizens of different states. But what law shall the courts apply in these cases? Swift v. Tyson in 1842, reversed ninety-six years later in Erie Railway v. Tomkins, was the first pass at this issue—an issue that lacks glamour but that may mean more to the actual day-to-day operation of our federal system in peoples' lives than any other. The case came into federal court under the court's diversity jurisdiction. The defendant, Tyson, issued a promissory note, payable in six months, to Norton and Keith in exchange for a parcel of land. Norton and Keith did not have title to the land they offered Tyson. Norton and Keith then exchanged the note with the plaintiff, Swift, as consideration for his canceling a debt they owed him. Swift received the note before it matured and without any knowledge of the defect of Norton and Keith's title to the land. When the note matured, Swift presented it to Tyson for payment, but Tyson refused payment. Swift then filed suit against Tyson in federal court in New York.

Tyson claimed that he was entitled to the same defense against Swift that he would be entitled to in an action against Norton and Keith. The judges of the circuit court divided on this question. The Supreme Court, in an opinion by Justice Story, stated that a holder of a negotiable note who receives the note for valuable consideration before it has matured and does not know of any defects in the original transaction is entitled to payment regardless of those defects. The question the Court considered was whether a preexisting debt was a valuable consideration for purposes of the preceding rule. Recent decisions by New York appellate courts indicated that a preexisting debt was not valuable consideration under New York's commercial law.

Tyson argued that section 34 of the Judiciary Act of 1789 required a federal court to apply the New York rule on negotiable instruments to this case. Section 34 provided "[t]hat the laws of the several states, except where the constitution, treaties or statutes of the United States shall otherwise require or provide, shall be regarded as rules of decision in trials at common law in the courts of the United States in cases where they apply." Because no provision of the Constitution or federal law or treaty controlled the issue in this case, *Tyson* argued that New York law must apply.

The Supreme Court disagreed. The Court held that the word "laws" in section 34 referred only to "the rules and enactments promulgated by the legislative authority [of a state], or long-established local customs having the force of law." The Court rested its holding on the ordinary meaning of the word "laws." The Court stated:

> In the ordinary use of language, it will hardly be contended, that the decisions of courts constitute laws. They are, at most, only evidence of what the laws are, and are not, of themselves, laws. They are often re-examined, reversed and qualified by the courts themselves, whenever they are found to be either defective, or ill-founded, or otherwise incorrect.[26]

The Court also argued that the importance of having uniform laws of commerce justified its decision not to apply the local rules of New York.

Because the New York rule concerning negotiable instruments was established by court decision, rather than statute, the Supreme Court found that the federal courts therefore were not bound by the rule. The Court concluded that a preexisting debt was a valuable consideration for a negotiable note, basing its decision on what was the prevailing rule in commercial law and on the practical advantages to commerce that it thought would be secured by the rule.

As we will see with the *Erie* case, the real-world consequences of Swift v. Tyson create a difficult problem. When two parties enter into a transaction that may be litigated, they cannot know in advance the rule that will be applied by the court because they cannot know in advance whether the suit will be brought in state or federal court. Furthermore, even if two states have the same legal rule, the one that got there legislatively will control federal litigation whereas the one that got there by judicial precedent will not. It is hard to think of any sensible reason for such a peculiar result. The result only makes sense if one accepts the idea that the common law is a real thing, the fixture of the heaven of juristic rectitude, rather than simply what we know it as today (i.e., as rules made by judges). If the common law is made in heaven by perfectionists, federal judges in Story's view must be closer to the gods than state judges and therefore should not defer to state common law.

Ex parte McCardle and Stripping the Federal Courts' Jurisdiction

One of the looming unresolved questions about checks and balances has always been the power of Congress to make "exceptions" to the jurisdiction of the Supreme Court. Congress doesn't like what the Court has to say about, to use modern examples, gay rights or Guantanamo. Congress can't "overrule" the Court, but can it just make an exception to its appellate jurisdiction in such a case? McCardle's 1868 case is the closest to an answer. A newspaper editor was arrested and held in military custody on charges that he published libelous articles against the Reconstruction government. He petitioned a U.S. circuit court for a writ of habeas corpus. The court found his confinement lawful. McCardle then appealed to the U.S. Supreme Court.

The Supreme Court was authorized to hear McCardle's appeal by an 1867 Act of Congress. That act amended the Judiciary Act of 1789 to provide, among other things, that a prisoner could appeal to the Supreme Court a circuit court's judgment on the prisoner's habeas petition. The government moved to dismiss the case, but the Supreme Court denied the motion. The Court then heard arguments on the merits. Before the Court rendered a judgment, however, Congress amended the Act of 1867 as follows:

> And be it further enacted, That so much of the act approved by February 5, 1867, entitled "An act to amend an act to establish the judicial courts of the United States,

approved September 24, 1789," as authorized an appeal from the judgment of the Circuit Court to the Supreme Court of the United States, or the exercise of any such jurisdiction by said Supreme Court, on appeals which have been, or may hereafter be taken, be, and the same is hereby repealed.[27]

The government moved again to dismiss. The Court granted the motion.

The Court held that it lacked jurisdiction to hear the case. The Court recognized that the Constitution confers appellate jurisdiction upon it "with such exceptions and under such regulations as Congress shall make." Because the act to repeal the Court's appellate jurisdiction in habeas cases was clearly an exception to the Court's jurisdiction, the Court found that it could not consider McCardle's appeal. The Court concluded by noting that only the jurisdiction conferred by the 1867 Act was repealed. The Court retained the jurisdiction it possessed under other acts of Congress. This concluding observation calls into question the actual meaning of McCardle. True, the Court *says* that Congress can take away the jurisdiction; however, the Court *holds* that Congress didn't take the jurisdiction away. It merely transferred it from one statute to another.

Murdock v. City of Memphis and the Independence of State Law

We saw in Martin v. Hunter's Lessee that the Supreme Court, speaking through Justice Story, firmly upheld the power of the U.S. Supreme Court over state *courts*. What that case left less clear was the power of the federal court over the substance of state law. In Swift v. Tyson, Justice Story also upheld federal power to supersede state law in diversity cases filed in federal courts. The missing part of the puzzle would be the deference owed to state law in a federal question case appealed from a state's high court to the federal Supreme Court. Murdock v. Memphis, in 1875, is that last piece.

The case came to the U.S. Supreme Court from the Supreme Court of Tennessee. Plaintiffs, Murdock and others, alleged that certain lands held by the city of Memphis were actually held by the city in trust for them. A Tennessee trial court dismissed the plaintiffs' claim, and the Supreme Court of Tennessee affirmed. Thirty years earlier, plaintiffs had conveyed land to the city of Memphis. They claimed that they conveyed the land to Memphis in trust for certain purposes, including building a Navy yard on the land. Memphis sold the land to the U.S. government for $20,000. Work was begun, but never completed, on a Navy yard. Ten years later, Congress passed an act ceding the land to the mayor and aldermen of Memphis for the city's use. Plaintiffs argued that this act of Congress gave the U.S. Supreme Court jurisdiction to review the decision of the Tennessee Supreme Court. Plaintiffs argued further that an 1867 Act of Congress authorized the Supreme Court to review not only the issues of federal law decided by the Tennessee Supreme Court, but also the issues of state law.

In 1867, Congress passed an act entitled "an act to amend 'An act to establish the judicial courts of the United States, approved September the 24th, 1789.'" The second section of the Act of 1867 was, with some exceptions, the same as the twenty-fifth section of the Judiciary Act of 1789. The relevant difference between the two statutes was that the Act of 1867 omitted the following clause concerning the Supreme Court's appellate jurisdiction, a clause that had been included in the original Judiciary Act:

> No other error shall be assigned or regarded as a ground of reversal in any such case as aforesaid than such as appears on the face of the record and immediately respects the before-mentioned questions of validity or construction of the said Constitution, treaties, statutes, commissions, or authorities in dispute.[28]

The omission of that clause suggested (1) that the Supreme Court's appellate review was not limited to considering issues of federal law; and (2) that the Supreme Court could now more fully investigate the proceedings of the state court decisions it reviewed. Those two suggestions raised four issues:

- Issue 1: Does the second section of the Act of 1867 repeal all or any part of the twenty-fifth section of the Judiciary Act?
- Issue 2: Does the Act of 1867 confer on the Supreme Court jurisdiction to decide all issues in a case where there is a federal question involved in the case, even if some of the questions do not involve federal law?
- Issue 3: Does the Constitution authorize Congress to confer such jurisdiction on the Supreme Court?
- Issue 4: Does the deletion of the phrase "such as appears on the face of the record" give the Supreme Court broader authority to look into the proceedings of the state court?

The Court answered the first question affirmatively. It found that the second section of the Act of 1867 completely replaced the twenty-fifth section of the Judiciary Act. The Court then answered the second question negatively. The Court held that if Congress had intended to confer the jurisdiction described in issue 2 upon the Court, then Congress would have used "plain, unmistakable language" to indicate its intent, because conferring such jurisdiction would reverse a policy that both Congress and the Court had followed since the founding of the republic. The Court also argued that its earlier decisions restricting its jurisdiction with respect to issues of state law had not rested entirely on the now-omitted clause of the Judiciary Act.

The Court cited a strong policy reason for not expanding its jurisdiction as plaintiffs proposed. The Court argued that if it had had jurisdiction to consider all the issues in a case once it acquired jurisdiction through the existence of a federal question, then all state cases could be reviewed in the Court. To get the case into the Supreme Court, a lawyer in state court would merely need to raise a federal question and have it decided against his client. The lawyer could do so even if he or she had no basis for raising the issue of federal law.

Furthermore, the Court noted that the policy reasons for granting it appellate jurisdiction over questions of federal law decided in state courts did not extend to granting the Court appellate jurisdiction over questions of state law. The purpose of conferring appellate jurisdiction on the Supreme Court to review state cases involving federal issues was to ensure uniformity of interpretation of federal law. That need does not exist with respect to state law issues involved in a case. A litigant whose rights depend on federal law should have the opportunity to have his or her rights judged in a federal court. No such right should exist with respect to questions of state law. Because the Court decided that Congress had not intended to expand its jurisdiction, the Court did not consider the question of whether such expansion would be constitutional. Nonetheless, the circumspection in the Court's opinion suggests that great constitutional doubts would be presented if Congress did actually attempt to give the Supreme Court authority over state law issues on appeal. Ever since that ruling, both Congress and the Court have avoided interpretations that might again raise that issue.

The Court then answered issue 4 affirmatively. The Court held that the omission quoted in issue 4 above in the Act of 1867 empowered it to consider the opinions issued in the state court proceeding and complete the record of proceedings in state courts to determine the basis of those courts' decisions. The Court argued that, by investigating state proceedings more thoroughly, it could sometimes avoid reversing a state court's judgment, even in cases in which the state court incorrectly decided the federal question. If there were sufficient state grounds to uphold the decision, then the Supreme Court would not reverse the state court's judgment. Applying its holding to the *Murdock* case, the Court affirmed the judgment of the Tennessee Supreme Court. The Court found that the question concerning the Congressional Act of 1854 was decided correctly, and the Court did not consider any issues of state law.

Justices Clifford and Swayne dissented. They found that the omission in the Act of 1867 clearly did expand the Court's jurisdiction to include state law issues. Justice Bradley also dissented. He did not believe that the Court had jurisdiction to hear the case. Bradley believed that the plaintiffs' claims rested entirely on the 1844 deed and thus did not involve any issue of federal law. Assuming the Court did have jurisdiction, however, Bradley would have found that the omission in the Act of 1867 expanded the Court's jurisdiction. Bradley noted that the Constitution gave the Court jurisdiction over *cases*, not *questions*. The Judiciary Act limited the Court's jurisdiction over cases to considerations of federal questions. Because the Act of 1867 removed the restrictive language, Bradley held that the Court now had its full constitutional jurisdiction over cases, that is, over all questions in cases. Had these dissents prevailed, the landscape of judicial power would be quite different after 1875. In effect, these three justices thought that Swift v. Tyson should apply in all cases, not just in diversity trials. The upshot would have been potential federal control of the common law in all matters—even in matters beyond the legislative powers of Congress. Such federalism might have seemed possible to those who thought that the common law was made, not found. Once the legal world came to see, however, that the common law was made by judges, not found by them, it would be a wholly different matter to give federal judges complete control. In this sense, Murdock was the beginning of the end for Swift v. Tyson.

Frank v. Mangum and the Great Writ

Until this case in 1915, the issues of federalism in Article III had mostly involved the role of federal courts in civil cases. The turmoil and conflicts of the twentieth century (the problems of world war, labor struggles, and civil rights foremost among them) began to raise more insistent problems of federal court involvement in state criminal cases. The constitutional logic of the cases mostly unfolded in the interstices of questions about jurisdiction, especially questions about the scope of the longstanding writ of habeas corpus.

Leo Frank was convicted of murder by a trial court in Georgia. Immediately after the conviction, Frank's attorney filed a motion for new trial. Two months later Frank's attorney amended the motion to include 103 different grounds. Those grounds included claims that disorder in the court during trial and expressions of hostility toward Frank prevented him from receiving a fair trial. The motion also asserted that the disorder in the court was so great that Frank was unable to be present in the courtroom when the verdict was read. The trial court denied Frank's motion for a new trial and the Georgia Supreme Court affirmed.

Frank then moved to set aside the verdict as a nullity. In this motion, Frank claimed that his absence from the court when the jury read the verdict was involuntary and thus deprived him of his right to trial by jury. The trial court again denied Frank's motion, and the Georgia Supreme Court again affirmed. Frank then applied to the U.S. District Court for the Northern District of Georgia for a writ of habeas corpus. The district court denied Frank's application, and Frank appealed the denial to the U.S. Supreme Court.

The Supreme Court affirmed. The Court noted that under the habeas corpus statute a prisoner could obtain relief only if he was held in custody in violation of the Constitution. The Court went on to state that under the Fourteenth Amendment a criminal prosecution satisfies the demands of the Constitution if—

- It is based on a constitutional law;
- The prosecution is conducted according to the settled course of judicial proceedings established by state law; and

- The established proceedings include notice, a hearing, and an opportunity to be heard before a court of competent jurisdiction.

Irregularities and erroneous rulings in the trial alone do not entitle a person to a writ of habeas corpus. Instead, a prisoner must show that the judgment under which he is detained was rendered by a court that did not have jurisdiction to render it. In this case, the Georgia trial court had jurisdiction when the trial began, but Frank contended that the disorder that occurred during the trial and his own absence when the verdict was read deprived the court of jurisdiction. The habeas corpus Act of 1867 authorized federal courts to look beyond the record of a prisoner's conviction to test the "jurisdiction" of the court that convicted the prisoner. The concept that constitutional violations divested the state court's jurisdiction was the magical syllogism that made the writ available.

The Supreme Court held that in reviewing Frank's conviction it could look not only at the proceedings of the trial court but also at the Georgia Supreme Court's review of the case. The Fourteenth Amendment prohibits *states* from denying persons due process of law. Therefore, if one agency of a state threatens to deprive a person of due process, but another agency prevents that deprivation, then the state has not violated the Fourteenth Amendment. Furthermore, a federal court may not issue a writ of habeas corpus until a prisoner has exhausted all remedies available to him or her under state law. Therefore, a federal court must look to all state law proceedings to determine whether it should issue a writ. For purposes of the Fourteenth Amendment, a prisoner has been denied due process of law only if his or her fundamental rights have "been taken from him arbitrarily or without the right to be heard according to the usual course of law in such cases."[29] The Due Process Clause of the Fourteenth Amendment does not require that state proceedings be perfect, and it does not authorize federal courts to substitute their judgment for the judgment of a state court.

A Georgia trial court and the Georgia Supreme Court both found that Frank's allegations of disorder during trial did not deprive him of a fair trial. The Supreme Court found that the state's corrective measures were sufficient to safeguard the rights of defendants. Defendants could move for a new trial and seek review of trial courts' rulings on their motions by the Georgia Supreme Court.

The Court also rejected Frank's claim that his absence from the courtroom when the jury read its verdict deprived the trial court of jurisdiction. The Court noted that under Georgia law a defendant could waive his right to be present while the jury read the verdict. In this case, however, Frank claimed that he did not waive his right to be present because his absence from the courtroom was involuntary. The Supreme Court held that Frank had waived his right to be present under Georgia law because his first motion for a new trial did not include among its grounds that his absence from the courtroom had been involuntary. The Court then reasoned that because the right to trial by jury was not (at that time) required by the Fourteenth Amendment, a state could limit the consequences of a trial court's error in conducting a trial by jury.

Justice Holmes, joined by Justice Hughes, dissented. Holmes argued that Frank's petition alleged such disorder and mob domination of the trial as to render the trial an empty proceeding. Holmes argued that because the Fourteenth Amendment guaranteed the right to a fair trial, Frank's petition for a writ of habeas corpus should be heard. Holmes pointed out that in a civil case the Supreme Court had held that the outcome of state corrective procedures did not decide the question of whether a person's federal rights had been violated. The same rule should apply with even greater force to criminal proceedings. Therefore, if the facts alleged in Frank's petition were true, the Georgia Supreme Court's decision that Frank should not receive a new trial could not restore the trial court's jurisdiction that was lost during mob domination. Although Frank was unsuccessful, the underlying logic of the decision contained potent tools for the future. Allowing fundamental unfairness to be litigated in habeas corpus petitions to a trial court gave these trial courts a functional power to hear appeals from state courts. Of course they aren't *called* appeals, but they have a similar effect. If the only federal review of state criminal convictions was a full-scale appeal to the U.S. Supreme Court, a rare, costly, and difficult process, state courts would have continued to enjoy practical autonomy in criminal cases.

Erie Railroad v. Tompkins and the Failure of the Federal Common Law

In 1938, ninety-six years after Swift v. Tyson, responding to both theoretical and practical concerns, the Supreme Court reversed that decision. Tompkins, a citizen of Pennsylvania, was injured by a passing freight train of the Erie Railroad Company, a New York corporation. Tompkins was injured in Pennsylvania while walking along a footpath that ran along the railroad tracks. He brought suit in the U.S. District Court for the Southern District of New York, claiming that Erie negligently maintained and operated its trains.

Erie claimed that, under Pennsylvania law, people who used longitudinal footpaths along railroad tracks were trespassers and that railroads were not liable for injuries to undiscovered trespassers unless the injuries were willful or caused by wanton negligence. Tompkins argued that federal courts were free to disregard Pennsylvania law in diversity cases and instead apply federal common law. The district court judge refused to apply Pennsylvania law, a jury returned a verdict in favor of Tompkins, and the Circuit Court of Appeals affirmed.

The Supreme Court reversed the judgment of the court of appeals, thereby overruling Swift v. Tyson. In *Swift* the Court held that section 34 of the Judiciary Act of 1789 required federal courts to apply state law in diversity cases only if the state law was expressed in a statute. Federal courts were not required to apply the law established by decisions of state appellate courts. The *Erie* Court advanced several arguments against the *Swift* doctrine. First, the Court noted that by giving federal courts the power to disregard the common law of the states, the courts gained a law-making power that the Constitution denied to Congress. Because the Constitution established a federal government with limited powers, it violated the Constitution for any branch of the government, including the judicial branch, to assume a power not granted to it by the Constitution.

The Court also noted that the *Swift* doctrine permitted litigants to invoke diversity jurisdiction to gain an advantage unavailable in purely intrastate disputes. In Black & White Taxicab & Transfer Co. v. Brown & Yellow Taxicab & Transfer Co., Brown & Yellow and the Louisville & Nashville Railroad formed a contract that gave Brown & Yellow the exclusive privilege of soliciting passenger and baggage transportation at the Bowling Green railroad station. The contract also provided that Black & White could be prevented from interfering with Brown & Yellow's exclusive privilege. Before forming the contract, both companies were incorporated in Kentucky. Because the contract they formed would have been invalid under the common law of Kentucky, Brown & Yellow reincorporated in Tennessee and the contract was executed in Tennessee. Brown & Yellow then brought suit in federal court in Kentucky to enjoin Black & White from soliciting business at the Bowling Green station. The court issued an injunction that the Supreme Court upheld. As *Black & White* illustrated, the *Swift* doctrine made it possible for noncitizens to discriminate against citizens by invoking diversity jurisdiction. Under *Swift*, the rights of the parties with respect to questions of common law depended on whether a case was decided in state or federal court. In a dispute between citizens, those questions would always be decided in state court, but in a dispute between a citizen and a noncitizen, the noncitizen could remove the case to federal court and thereby gain an advantage unavailable to a citizen in the same position as the noncitizen. Thus, noncitizens could gain an advantage in litigation that citizens could not. The result was a kind of abusive "forum shopping."

While the *Swift* doctrine had created unfair results, countervailing positive results had not happened. Although Justice Story in the *Swift* Court had hoped that establishing a federal common law would create greater uniformity among state courts, state variance had continued. Whatever uniformity came about in the twentieth century was a result of legislative cooperation rather than the possible modeling effect of a federal common law.

The Court also relied on Charles Warren's article "New Light on the History of the Federal Judiciary Act of 1789" in which Warren claimed to have found new documentary evidence that showed that the *Swift* Court's reading of section 34 was incorrect.[30]

For all the reasons stated above, the Court overruled *Swift* and held that:

Except in matters governed by the Federal Constitution or by acts of Congress, the law to be applied in any case is the law of the state. And whether the law of the state shall be declared by its Legislature in a statute or by its highest court in a decision is not a matter of federal concern.[31]

In overruling *Swift*, the Court stated that it did not find section 34 of the Judiciary Act to be unconstitutional. Rather, the Court found that federal courts' misreading of section 34 had caused them to exceed their constitutional authority.

Justice Butler dissented. He found that the majority's decision did declare section 34, as construed by the federal courts, to be unconstitutional. As a result of the majority's decision, Congress was now powerless to prescribe rules of decision for federal courts when deciding issues of common law. Justice Butler wrote that it was unnecessary to have reached such important questions because there was evidence in this case that Tompkins was guilty of contributory negligence and that the lower courts' decisions should be reversed on that ground.

Justice Reed concurred in part but dissented from that part of the majority opinion that held that the *Swift* doctrine was unconstitutional. He argued that the result was proper under section 34 of the Judiciary Act, but Congress was free, if it chose, to allow the federal courts to develop a federal common law. It is often carelessly said that *Erie* marks the end of the federal common law, whereas it simply removes the federal common law from diversity cases. Federal common law still exists, not without controversy, for some situations, mainly those involving private transactions with the federal government.[32]

Fay v. Noia and the Modern Scope of Habeas Corpus

People often refer to the Warren Court, by which they usually mean to identify a spirit of activist commitment to social justice during Earl Warren's Chief Justiceship from 1953 to 1969. A large part of that activism was in the federal court review of state convictions. As a practical matter, that review simply could not have occurred if it had been limited to exercises of the Supreme Court's appellate jurisdiction. In one year, the Supreme Court hears fewer cases, by far, than a single state court judge in felony court. Faye v. Noia, in 1963, marked the transformation of habeas corpus, growing from the slender theory first developed in 1915 in Frank v. Mangum, which made search warrants and *Miranda* warnings a fact of life.

A New York state court convicted Charles Noia, Santo Caminito, and Frank Bonino of murder. The only evidence the state presented against the defendants was their signed confessions. Caminito and Bonino appealed their convictions. Although their direct appeals within the state court system were unsuccessful, both obtained release from prison during subsequent legal proceedings that revealed their confessions were coerced in violation of the Fourteenth Amendment. Noia did not appeal his conviction. He did file a petition for a writ of habeas corpus in the U.S. District Court for the Southern District of New York. Although the district court found that Noia's confession was also coerced, the court denied Noia's petition because Noia had failed to appeal. The habeas corpus statute provided that "[a]n application for a writ of habeas corpus in behalf of a person in custody pursuant to the judgment of a State court shall not be granted unless it appears that the applicant has exhausted the remedies available in the courts of the State. . . ."[33] The district court held that Noia's failure to appeal was a failure to exhaust remedies available to him in state court. The federal court of appeals reversed the district court and ordered that Noia's conviction be set aside and that he be released from custody. Affirming, the Supreme Court held that a prisoner's failure to pursue a state remedy that is no longer available at the time he or she applies for a writ of habeas corpus will not bar a federal court from granting habeas relief. The Court first reviewed the history of habeas corpus in England and the United States and found that writs of habeas corpus traditionally had been available to any prisoner whose detention violated fundamental law. The Court specifically rejected claims that habeas corpus had been limited to executive detentions imposed by courts that lacked jurisdiction. The Court then stated that its own precedent established that a prisoner who had been convicted of a crime in state court could seek habeas relief in federal court on the grounds that his or her confession had been coerced.

Turning to the question of whether Noia had failed to exhaust state remedies as required by statute, the Court found that the requirement of exhausting state remedies was a principle of comity, which required it to defer action on habeas corpus petitions until another court sharing jurisdiction over the case completed its review of the case. Federal courts thus have jurisdiction to consider violations of prisoners' federal rights even though state courts may also review those violations. Although the Supreme Court in Frank v. Mangum had denied a prisoner a writ of habeas corpus because the prisoner's conviction had already been reviewed by a state appellate court, the Court later held in Moore v. Dempsey that the conclusions of state courts were not conclusive with respect to federal rights. Therefore, no state proceeding can take away a federal court's jurisdiction to consider a prisoner's claim that his or her federal rights were violated.

The limits on the Supreme Court's appellate review of state court decisions differs from the limits on federal courts' habeas jurisdiction. Appellate review concerns the judgments of state courts. In contrast, habeas corpus jurisdiction does not require a court judgment, but only the detention of a prisoner. Therefore, the existence of adequate and independent state grounds for a conviction affects the Supreme Court's jurisdiction on direct review of a case but does not affect its jurisdiction on habeas review. Thus, the Court held that while a prisoner's procedural default in state court could bar direct federal review, that default would not ordinarily bar federal habeas review. The Court also held that a prisoner's failure to seek timely certiorari in the Supreme Court from an adverse state judgment would not bar habeas relief.

The Court's holding did leave some discretion to federal judges to deny a writ of habeas corpus to an applicant "who has deliberately bypassed the orderly procedure of the state courts and in so doing has forfeited his state court remedies." By the 1990s, both statutory provisions and case law had significantly modified this standard and greatly restricted a state prisoner's use of habeas corpus in cases in which state procedures have been ignored or inadequately used.[34]

Justice Harlan, joined by Justices Clark and Stewart, dissented. His dissent in this case is one of the classic statements of his philosophy of judicial power and contributed to his recognition as the leading conservative critic of the jurisdictional aspects of the Warren Court. Harlan reviewed the history of habeas corpus in the United States and found that the majority's holding far exceeded the relief traditionally available. Before 1915, the writ of habeas corpus was available only where the court that had sentenced a defendant did not have jurisdiction to do so. Habeas relief was expanded in the period from 1915 to 1953 to permit federal courts to consider whether state courts had given prisoners adequate opportunities to raise their claims of federal rights. Habeas relief was expanded again in 1953 in the case of Brown v. Allen. In that case, the Court held that where a prisoner raised a constitutional claim in state court and alleged that the state court's determination of his or her constitutional claim was incorrect, the prisoner could seek habeas relief in federal court. In Daniels v. Allen, a case decided the same year, the Court held that a prisoner's failure to follow state procedural requirements could constitute adequate state ground for a conviction and that habeas relief was not available in such cases.

Harlan also argued that the majority opinion gave federal courts power beyond Article III. In his view, if an adequate state ground for a conviction bars direct review by the Supreme Court, then that same ground must also bar collateral review by federal district courts. In either direct or collateral review, the state judgment may be overturned. The procedural differences between direct review and habeas review should not alter the constitutional relationships between state and federal courts. In many respects, comparing the dissent with the majority on this exact point reveals much about the development of Article III. Harlan's view seems ironclad so far as the constitutional text is concerned: there is "one supreme Court." But the practical realities of using federal courts to enforce the rule of law, which is the point of the whole project, requires something like the expanded writ of habeas corpus. Is it to Harlan and the letter, or Justice Brennan and the spirit?

Younger v. Harris and Federal Court Injunctions against State Trials

Habeas corpus could shortcut the process of federal review in state criminal cases. What would be even more effective would be a pretrial federal order preventing trial in the first place. Historically, such orders had been shunned as something like an insult to the integrity of state courts. Several celebrated cases during the Civil Rights Era, however, had probed at the limits of this traditional prohibition. In 1971, two years after Earl Warren's departure, the Supreme Court revisited and reinvigorated the ban. Harris was indicted in California state court for violating California's Criminal Syndicalism Act. That statute prohibited, among other things, advocating or teaching violent methods to change the political system or system of industrial ownership. Harris then filed a complaint in federal district court seeking to enjoin Younger, the Los Angeles District Attorney, from prosecuting him. Harris claimed that the prosecution and the Act itself violated his First and Fourteenth Amendment rights to freedom of speech and press. Dean, Hirsch, and Broslawsky intervened as plaintiffs. Dean and Hirsch claimed that Harris's prosecution would inhibit their activities, in the Progressive Labor Party, of peacefully advocating socialism. Broslawsky claimed that Harris's prosecution inhibited him as a college history teacher from teaching the doctrines of Karl Marx. A three-judge federal district court panel held that the Criminal Syndicalism Act was void for vagueness and overbreadth and enjoined Younger from prosecuting Harris.

The Supreme Court reversed. First, the Court held that the three intervenors, Dean, Hirsch, and Broslawsky, did not have standing to seek an injunction of Harris's prosecution. None of them had been threatened with prosecution, nor did they claim that prosecution was likely or even possible. Because Harris had been indicted, however, he did have standing to seek an injunction.

The Court then considered whether an injunction should issue. The starting point of its analysis was the Anti-Injunction Act, which provides that "[a] court of the United States may not grant an injunction to stay proceedings in a State court except as expressly authorized by Act of Congress, or where necessary in aid of its jurisdiction, or to protect or effectuate its judgments."[35] A judicially created exception also permitted federal courts to stay state proceedings in cases in which the person to be prosecuted would suffer irreparable damage if the state proceedings continued. The irreparable damage had to be "both great and immediate" and had to involve damage beyond "the cost, anxiety, and inconvenience of having to defend against a single prosecution."[36]

The Court described strong policies that supported limiting the ability of federal courts to stay state court proceedings. First, it was a basic doctrine of equity—and the historical rules about injunctions had been articulated in courts of equity—that an injunction should not issue if a party has an adequate remedy in the ordinary law courts. The courts in which criminal cases are tried are courts of "law" not "equity." Second, principles of comity and federalism require that federal courts allow state courts to function independently. Comity is the concept of mutual respect among sovereigns, both internationally and state to state. Also, permitting federal courts to stay proceedings in state courts based on the possible unconstitutionality of a state law would expand the power of judicial review beyond the limits set by Marbury v. Madison. As the *Younger* Court read *Marbury*, the power of judicial review is based on judges' duty to decide actual cases in conformity with the Supremacy Clause. An unconstitutional law must be struck down because the Constitution is the supreme law of the United States. The power of judicial review does not, however, give federal judges the right to examine state statutes for unconstitutionality outside the context of a real dispute. The dispute between Harris and California was not yet ripe for the Court to consider it a real dispute rather than a potential one.

In *Younger*, none of the statutory factors permitted a federal court to stay the state court proceedings; nor did the Court find that Harris would suffer irreparable injury by being forced to defend against prosecution in state court. Harris would have an opportunity to raise a constitutional challenge to the California law in state court, and there was no evidence that the prosecution was brought in bad faith or that Harris would be subjected to repeated prosecutions. The Court therefore reversed the judgment of the district court.

Bivens v. Six Unknown Named Agents of Federal Bureau of Narcotics: The Constitution as Sword Rather Than Shield

Although Younger v. Harris restricted federal court intervention in state criminal cases, another 1971 decision gave, for the first time, a strong reading to Article III's jurisdiction "arising under this Constitution." Federal narcotics agents arrested Bivens in his home, searched his home, and later subjected him to a strip search at a federal courthouse. Bivens filed suit in federal district court claiming that the narcotics agents executed the arrest and search without a warrant and used unreasonable force in making the arrest. The Supreme Court read the complaint as claiming that the agents made the arrest without probable cause. Bivens sought $15,000 in damages from each agent. The district court dismissed the complaint for failure to state a cause of action, and the court of appeals affirmed.

The Supreme Court reversed. In doing so, it rejected the government's argument that Bivens's remedy against federal agents should be limited to the remedy he could obtain in a tort action against a private citizen. The Court first noted that the Fourth Amendment's protections against unreasonable search and seizure applied to federal officers regardless of the protections of state law. Second, the Court noted that the interests protected by state trespass law differed from the interests protected by the Fourth Amendment. A citizen may call upon the police to protect his or her rights against fellow citizens, but only the courts can protect a citizen against the police. Furthermore, although the states may modify their trespass laws, states are powerless to expand or to contract the protections the Fourth Amendment offers against federal officers.

The Court then held that a federal agent's violation of the Fourth Amendment gave rise to a cause of action for damages. The Court stated, "Historically, damages have been regarded as the ordinary remedy for an invasion of personal interests in liberty." The Court recognized that special factors might sometimes counsel hesitation in recognizing this self-enforcing effect of the Constitution.

Justice Harlan concurred in the judgment. Like the majority, Harlan rejected the view that courts are unable to provide remedies for violations of constitutional rights in the absence of congressional action. Harlan noted that the Court had authorized damages suits for violations of federal statutes, even where those statutes did not provide for private causes of action. Because the judiciary has a special duty to guard constitutional rights, Harlan believed that the freedom of the judiciary to craft remedies for violations of those rights should be at least as great as the judiciary's power to provide remedies for violations of statute. Harlan also argued that, in the absence of a damages remedy, Bivens could not vindicate his Fourth Amendment rights. He was not in a position to obtain an injunction preventing his arrest and the search of his home and person. The federal government is immune from suit. And because Bivens appeared to be innocent of narcotics crimes, he could not be prosecuted and the right to exclude illegal evidence would have nothing to which to apply.

Justice Harlan concluded by addressing the argument that permitting private damages actions against federal officers would waste judicial resources. Harlan first argued that it was unlikely that a great volume of lawsuits would follow the Court's decision. Second, Harlan argued that the importance of Fourth Amendment rights justified the use of judicial resources. Because the Court allowed stockholders who were defrauded by misleading proxies to pursue damages actions, denying the same remedy to people whose Fourth Amendment rights were violated would express the judgment that Fourth Amendment rights are less important than the stockholder rights.

Northern Pipeline Construction Co. v. Marathon Pipe Line Co. and Judges Outside Article III

In 1978, Congress enacted the Bankruptcy Act, which created special bankruptcy courts in each federal judicial circuit. Under the Act, bankruptcy judges were to be appointed by the president, with the advice and consent of the Senate, for fourteen-year terms. Bankruptcy judges were subject to removal by the judicial council of their circuit for incompetence, misconduct, neglect of duty, or physical or mental disability. The salaries of bankruptcy judges were set by statute and subject to adjustment. These provisions (above all, the lack of tenure during "good Behaviour") meant that bankruptcy judges could not be the judges empowered by Article III. The Act, however, gave bankruptcy courts jurisdiction over all civil proceedings arising under the federal bankruptcy laws and *related* cases.

Northern Pipeline Construction Co. filed a petition for reorganization in the U.S. Bankruptcy Court for the District of Minnesota. Northern Pipeline also filed suit in that court against Marathon Pipe Line Co. alleging non-bankruptcy claims for breaches of contract and warranty, misrepresentation, coercion, and duress. Marathon moved to dismiss the suit on the ground that the Bankruptcy Act violated Article III of the Constitution by conferring Article III power on judges who lacked life tenure and protection against reductions in salaries. The U.S. government intervened to defend the Bankruptcy Act. The bankruptcy court denied the motion to dismiss, and the district court reversed.

The Supreme Court affirmed the district court's judgment dismissing the case. Justice Brennan, writing for a plurality of the justices, held that Article III required that the judicial power of the United States be exercised by judges who have Article III attributes, namely, life tenure and a salary that cannot be diminished. The purpose of those Article III provisions, they said, was to ensure the independence of the judiciary from the other branches of government.

In an earlier line of cases, the Supreme Court had recognized a category of federal tribunals known as "legislative courts"—courts created outside Article III to deal with specialized subject matters. Northern and the United States argued that the bankruptcy courts could have been created as "legislative courts." Therefore, Congress did not impermissibly grant Article III jurisdiction to non–Article III judges. The plurality rejected this argument. The plurality held that Congress had authority to establish legislative courts only in three circumstances: (1) territorial and District of Columbia courts; (2) courts-martial; and (3) courts to adjudicate public rights. Congress's power to create territorial courts stemmed from its authority granted by Article IV to exercise the complete power of the government in U.S. territories not yet admitted as states. Because Article I gave Congress the complete power of government over the District of Columbia, the plurality held that Congress could establish legislative courts for the District of Columbia. Similarly, Congress also has the power to establish legislative courts-martial because the Constitution grants control over the armed forces to Congress and the president. The court defined "public rights" as matters between citizens and the government that involve the performance of the constitutional functions of either the executive or the legislative branch. Congress is free to establish legislative courts to resolve public rights disputes, because Congress could leave the resolution of such disputes entirely to members of the legislative or executive branch. Furthermore, because the doctrine of sovereign immunity permits Congress to refuse to allow suits against the government entirely, Congress is free to attach conditions to its consent to be sued.

In contrast to public rights cases, private rights cases historically have been recognized as being within judicial power. The Court acknowledged that it had not provided a clear test to distinguish all public rights cases from private rights cases. At a minimum, however, public rights cases must be between the government and others. The dispute between Northern and Marathon was not a public rights case because it was a dispute between two private parties. Although the discharge of debt may be a public right, related contract disputes do not involve public rights. Furthermore, the plurality stated, the Constitution did not confer an exceptional power on Congress over bankruptcy-related disputes in the way it did over territories, the District of Columbia, and the military. Northern argued, however, that because the Constitution gave Congress the power to establish "uniform Laws on the subject of Bankruptcies throughout the United States," Congress could therefore establish legislative courts to resolve bankruptcy disputes. The plurality responded that Northern's argument could apply to any of Congress's constitutional powers. Thus, if the Court were to accept legislative courts in bankruptcies, the Court would be forced to accept legislative courts to decide issues related to any subject over which Congress may legislate. That recognition would remove all federal subject matter from Article III jurisdiction.

Northern also argued that the Bankruptcy Act was constitutional because the bankruptcy courts were merely adjuncts to the district courts. While the plurality recognized that Congress could create adjuncts to Article III courts in certain circumstances, Congress's power to create adjuncts was subject to two limitations. First, Congress's power to create adjuncts is strongest in situations in which Congress creates adjuncts to adjudicate congressionally created rights. Second, Congress must limit the role of adjuncts so that the "essential attributes" of judicial power remain with an Article III court. In the Bankruptcy Act, however, Congress assigned to adjuncts the power to adjudicate both congressionally and state-created rights, such as the breach of contract action in the present case. Furthermore, Congress granted the bankruptcy adjuncts greater authority than it had granted other adjuncts who adjudicated only congressionally created rights. Therefore, the plurality concluded that the Bankruptcy Act impermissibly removed most, if not all, of "the essential attributes of the judicial power" from Article III district courts.

The Court affirmed the judgment of the district court in 1982 but stayed its judgment for a few months to give Congress an opportunity to recast the statute. After an embarrassing delay of two years, generating much uncertainty, Congress finally decided, in effect, to provide that bankruptcy judges should hold hearings and prepare findings primarily for final approval by district judges, thus making the bankruptcy judges "adjunct." (The bankruptcy judges also retain direct authority over the management and control of the bankrupt's property.)[37]

Justice Rehnquist, joined by Justice O'Connor, concurred in the judgment. While they agreed that the portions of the Bankruptcy Act that authorized bankruptcy courts to hear Northern's lawsuit against Marathon were unconstitutional, they did not accept the broader discussion of the circumstances in which Congress could create non–Article III courts. Purely as a matter of clarity, this is unfortunate because the plurality opinion was perhaps the first reasonably precise delineation of what legislative courts could be.

Justice White, joined by Chief Justice Burger and Justice Powell, dissented. White noted that almost all issues in bankruptcy proceedings involve issues of state law because these issues concern sales, wages, rent, and other issues governed by state law. There is no way to separate the bankruptcy proceedings from state law issues. The issues of state law would not ordinarily be heard by an Article III judge, but rather by a state court judge. As a result, the Bankruptcy Act's provisions did not seriously diminish the power of Article III judges.

White then reviewed the Court's precedents in the area of legislative courts and concluded that the plurality's attempt to define in what circumstances legislative courts may operate was unsatisfactory. Rather than a clear rule limiting the range of legislative courts, White believed that the Court must engage in a much less determinate process of balancing the values of an independent judiciary embodied in Article III against "competing constitutional values and legislative responsibilities." In making that balance, the Court must determine how much Article III values will be undermined by permitting legislative courts. Some of the factors the Court should consider are whether a decision of a legislative court can be appealed to an Article III court and whether the issues the legislative courts deal with are likely to be of little interest to the political branches. Where appellate review is available and the subject matter is of little political interest, legislative courts probably will not undermine Article III values. Because both of those factors were present in the bankruptcy courts, White did not believe the Bankruptcy Act was unconstitutional.

The larger issues of process raised by Justice White's dissent are central to the future of the federal court system. The details of Article III, section 2, are tied by language and history to a legal world that no longer exists. It was inspired by a common-law legal world driven largely by models of private rights recognized by tradition. Marbury v. Madison, in form at least, was presented as a case about Marbury's property interest in the commission, not as a case about the nature of democracy in a new world. The approach in the plurality opinion did not command a majority so the law in action has remained less than perfectly clear.[38]

Michigan v. Long and Adequate State Grounds

As the Supreme Court in the 1980s began to restrict criminal procedure rights that it had expanded during the 1960s, there was some movement among state courts to broaden their own interpretations of rights in their own state constitutions. The intersection between federal retrenchment and state elaboration put pressure on the adequate state ground doctrine as initially articulated in Murdock v. Memphis. Long's case brought a reconsideration of the relationship between state constitutional interpretation and the U.S. Supreme Court in 1983. Michigan police officers observed David Long driving rapidly and erratically. After he swerved off the road into a ditch, the officers approached the car. Meeting them at the rear of the car, he refused to respond to some of the police officers' requests and appeared to be under the influence of drugs or alcohol. When Long began walking away from the police, back to his car, the officers noticed a large hunting knife on the floorboard of the driver's side of the car. The police then subjected Long to a frisk for weapons, finding none. The police then shone a flashlight in the car and noticed something protruding from under the armrest on the front seat. The object turned out to be a pouch that contained marijuana. The officers arrested Long for possession of marijuana, impounded his car, and made an inventory search of the trunk. They found seventy-five pounds of marijuana in the trunk.

In the resulting state court criminal trial, Long moved to suppress the marijuana found in the passenger compartment and trunk of his car. The trial court denied the motion, and the Michigan Court of Appeals affirmed. The Michigan Supreme Court then reversed, holding that the search of the passenger compartment exceeded the authority of police to conduct a limited search on a basis less than probable cause. The operative language in the Michigan Supreme Court's opinion read, "We hold, therefore, that the deputies' search of the vehicle was proscribed by the Fourth Amendment to the United States Constitution and art. I, § 11 of the Michigan Constitution." The court's failure to distinguish clearly between state and federal law raised the issue whether the action was one "arising" under federal law or state law.

The state appealed to the U.S. Supreme Court. Long argued that the Supreme Court lacked jurisdiction to hear the case because the Michigan Supreme Court ordered the suppression of the marijuana on the basis of both the U.S. and the Michigan constitutions. Even if the Michigan Supreme Court decided the federal issue incorrectly, his dismissal in Michigan was inevitable. The federal decision was, therefore, immaterial to the outcome of the actual case because there was an "adequate and independent state ground" for its judgment. The Supreme Court disagreed, holding that it had jurisdiction to hear the case and reversing the Michigan Supreme Court's decision. The Court began by reviewing the various methods it had used in previous decisions to determine whether a state court decision rested on adequate and independent state grounds. The Court stated that all of those methods were unsatisfactory in some way. First, the Court rejected the method of undertaking its own examination of state law. The Court found that it was too unfamiliar with the laws of the fifty states and parties too often failed to fully brief state law issues to make this alternative workable. Second, the Court found that remanding cases to state courts for those courts to clarify their decisions was inefficient and placed too heavy a burden on state courts. Third, the Court rejected the possibility of dismissing all state cases in which the bases of the state courts' decisions were unclear, because dismissing those cases would hamper the Court's efforts to ensure uniformity in the interpretation of federal law.

The Court then adopted the following test:

> [W]hen, as in this case, a state court decision fairly appears to rest primarily on federal law, or to be interwoven with the federal law, and when the adequacy and independence of any possible state law ground is not clear from the face of the opinion, we will accept as the most reasonable explanation that the state court decided the case the way it did because it believed that federal law required it to do so.[39]

Thus, where a state court decision appears to depend on issues of federal law, the Supreme Court will presume that it does so in the absence of a clear statement to the contrary.

Applying the rule to the present case, the Court found that the Michigan Supreme Court's decision rested on the Fourth Amendment, rather than on any state law ground. Although the Court recognized that the Michigan Supreme Court had cited the Michigan constitution in its opinion, the Court found that the Michigan Supreme Court's interpretation of the Michigan constitution was not independent of its interpretation of the U.S. Constitution. The Court therefore concluded that "we have jurisdiction in the absence of a plain statement that the decision below rested on an adequate and independent state ground."

The Court then concluded that the police officers' search of the passenger compartment of Long's car was permitted as a protective search for weapons under the Fourth Amendment.

Justices Brennan and Marshall dissented on the substance of the Fourth Amendment but agreed that the Supreme Court had jurisdiction. Although they did not embrace the larger framework of the Court's jurisdictional analysis, they accepted that, in this particular case, the Michigan court had interpreted its own constitution as it did because it thought the result was compelled by the U.S. Constitution. In consequence, the state ground was not "independent."

Justice Stevens dissented. He argued that the Court did not have jurisdiction and criticized the majority's jurisdictional test. Stevens first stated that there was no precedent to support the majority's test. In the past, Stevens stated, the Court had always (1) remanded the case to state court for clarification; (2) attempted to determine on its own whether there were adequate and independent state grounds; or (3) presumed that there were adequate and independent state grounds. Thus, Stevens reasoned, if the Court now rejects the first two alternatives, it should, as a matter of stare decisis, adopt the third. Stevens also argued that the third alternative best advanced the policies of respecting state courts, avoiding advisory opinions, and conserving federal judicial resources.

Furthermore, Stevens did not believe that the *Long* case was one in which Supreme Court review was important. According to Stevens, "in reviewing the decisions of state courts, the primary role of this Court is to make sure that persons who seek to *vindicate* federal rights have been fairly heard." Because Long's rights had not been violated by Michigan, Stevens did not believe that Supreme Court review was warranted, even if the Michigan Supreme Court afforded Long more protection than he deserved under federal law. In response to the majority's contention that review was needed to ensure the uniformity of federal law, Stevens countered that the need for uniformity often gives way to the Court's requirement against rendering advisory opinions. Stevens's dissent makes it possible to frame the question with precision. Is the purpose of appellate jurisdiction to promote uniformity, as the majority says, or is it simply to protect federal rights? To put the same question a slightly different way, should the federal courts be concerned if the Michigan state courts err in overprotecting federal rights? This is in many ways the same policy question that the Court dealt with in the movement from *Swift* to *Erie*. A consistent answer about the importance, or not, of uniformity has so far eluded the Court.

Webster v. Doe: Are Courts Essential to Due Process?

The deep and enduring question about Article III is how it fits into the rest of the Constitution. Over time, we have seen what the courts *can* do, and, often, *how* they must go about doing what it is that they do. We have come to think of this as defining the rule of law. But behind these mechanics remains the one question: can Congress authorize the government to act without allowing the courts to intervene? Nothing in the language of Article III answers this question. McCardle's case, after the Civil War, sidestepped the somewhat easier question of whether Congress could remove the Supreme Court from appellate review of the lower courts. The Supreme Court has been equally assiduous in avoiding a definitive answer to that question, as illustrated by the 1988 decision in Webster v. Doe. John Doe was a gay man who worked without problem at the Central

Intelligence Agency (CIA) for several years. He received excellent work evaluations and was promoted from clerk-typist to covert electronics technician. After he voluntarily informed a CIA security officer that he was a homosexual, the CIA placed him on leave and began an investigation to determine whether his homosexuality posed a risk to national security. Although a polygraph test revealed that Doe truthfully stated that he had not disclosed security information to any of his sexual partners, the director fired him after he refused to resign.

Doe sued the director in U.S. District Court for the District of Columbia alleging that the director violated a statute known as the Administrative Procedure Act (APA). Doe also alleged that his termination violated his constitutional rights to property, liberty, privacy, due process, and equal protection. He sought to be reinstated, or, in the alternative, to be placed on paid administrative leave pending a formal evaluation of his termination. If the director then decided to terminate him, Doe maintained that the director must provide a statement of his reasons for doing so. As a legal problem, what Doe was seeking is pretty minimal due process. The principal problem is not whether these administrative actions were constitutional in the abstract: they aren't. The problem is whether any court has jurisdiction to hear his substantive claim.

Section 102(c) of the National Security Act (NSA) provides that "the Director of Central Intelligence may, *in his discretion*, terminate the employment of any officer or employee of the Agency whenever he shall deem such termination necessary or advisable in the interests of the United States . . ." (italics added). On the other hand, section 706 of the APA provides for judicial review of the actions of administrative agencies where, among other things, the agencies act in a manner that is "arbitrary, capricious, [or] an abuse of discretion" or the agencies act "without observance of procedure required by law." That review is limited by section 701(a) of the Procedure Act, which prohibits judicial review if such review is precluded by statute or if the agency action is committed to agency discretion by law. The Court concluded that the language and structure of section 102(a) of the NSA committed the termination of CIA employees to agency discretion. The express language of section 102(a) permitted the director to terminate a CIA employee whenever the director *deemed* termination necessary or advisable in the interests of the United States. Because the director was not obligated to show that termination actually was necessary or advisable, the Court concluded that there was no basis on which a reviewing court could review the director's decision. The Court also noted that the NSA as a whole shows great deference to the director. The Court therefore concluded that there was no jurisdiction of the alleged violations of the APA.

But the Court went on to hold that the NSA did not preclude judicial review of Doe's constitutional claims. The Court stated that "where Congress intends to preclude judicial review of constitutional claims its intent to do so must be clear." The Court adopted this heightened requirement for constitutional claims, in part, to avoid what it called the "serious constitutional question" of a statute precluding judicial review of a conceivably valid constitutional claim. The Court concluded that permitting constitutional claims to go forward against the director would not pose any greater risk to national security than other kinds of litigation from which the director had not been exempted and that the trial courts could protect the nation's secrets by carefully controlling the trial and discovery process.

Justice O'Connor dissented from the majority's holding that Doe could pursue his constitutional claims. The director's powers ultimately flow from the president's constitutional authority to conduct international relations. In her view, Congress should be able to insulate the director from judicial interference with a power granted to the president by the Constitution.

Justice Scalia's dissent was wide-ranging. His fundamental challenge was to the idea that courts should be presumed to have power to review judicial action. He called upon various specific doctrines insulating governments from the courts: the political question doctrine, sovereign immunity, official immunity, prudential limitations on equitable powers, and respect for the functions of other branches of government. Scalia concludes by arguing that the majority's decision gives the judiciary too much power over issues of intelligence gathering, endangers national security by permitting the inevitable discovery that comes with litigation, and calls into question whether there are any executive decisions that are immune from judicial review. And it is that latter question the Court avoids for the time being, until, that is, Congress says so in so many words.

NOTES

1. John Frank, "Historical Bases of the Federal Judicial System," 13 *Law and Contemporary Problems* 2 (1948).

2. Mary Bilden, "The Origin of the Appeal in America," 48 *Hastings L.J.* 913 (1997).

3. Edward Corwin, "The 'Higher Law' Background of American Constitutional Law, Part I," 42 *Harv. L. Rev.* 149 (1928).

4. The Supreme Court itself has made an authoritative review of this history in Hendry v. Moore, 318 U.S. 133 (1943).

5. Henry J. Bourguignon, *The First Federal Court* (Philadelphia: American Philosophical Society, 1977). See generally, Eric Freedman, "Why Constitutional Lawyers and Historians Should Take a Fresh Look at the Emergence of the Constitution from the Colonial Period: The Case of the Drafting of the Articles of Confederation," 60 *Tenn. L. Rev.* 783 (1993).

6. Akhil Amar, *America's Constitution: A Biography* 207–08 (New York: Random House, 2005).

7. 1 Max Farrand, *The Records of the Federal Convention of 1787* 20–23 (New Haven, CT: Yale University Press, 1966).

8. 1 Farrand, *The Records of the Federal Convention of 1787*, 124–25.

9. The Federalist No. 76, at 457 (Alexander Hamilton) (New York: Signet, Clinton Rossiter ed., 1999).

10. 2 Farrand, *The Records of the Federal Convention of 1787*, 46.

11. 2 Farrand, *The Records of the Federal Convention of 1787*, 430–31.

12. Both actions were taken without dissent and with no substantive discussion. 2 Farrand, *The Records of the Federal Convention of 1787*, 431, 433.

13. Charles Warren, "New Light on the History of the Judiciary Act of 1789," 37 *Harv. L. Rev.* 49 (1923).

14. Alexander Hamilton, after conceding that the jury argument by opponents met "with most success," goes on to catalog in extreme detail the complexity of the problem and the variation from state to state. The Federalist No. 83, at 501–02.

15. Wilfrid J. Ritz, *Rewriting the History of the Judiciary Act of 1789* 5–6 (Norman, OK, and London: University of Oklahoma Press, 1990) (This work was edited after Professor Ritz's death by Wythe Holt and L. H. LaRue).

16. The Federalist No. 80, at 474–76 (Alexander Hamilton) (New York: Signet, Clinton Rossiter ed., 1999).

17. The Constitution "listed the judiciary last among the branches. The textual order of the Constitution's first three article made both conceptual and democratic sense." Amar, *America's Constitution*, 208.

18. David Currie, *The Constitution in Congress* 47 (Chicago: University of Chicago Press, 1997).

19. 28 U.S.C. § 1332(a).

20. Section 9 of the Judiciary Act, now 28 U.S.C. § 1350.

21. Act of February 16, 1875, 18 Stat. 315.

22. See, generally, Thomas Rowe and Kenneth Sibley, "Beyond Diversity: Federal Multiparty, Multiforum Jurisdiction," 135 *U. Pa. L. Rev.* 7 (1986).

23. Osborn v. Bank of U.S., 22 U.S. 738, 822 (1824).

24. *Id.* at 823.

25. *Id.* at 857.

26. Swift v. Tyson, 41 U.S. 1, 18 (1842).

27. Act of March 27, 1868, ch. 34 § 2, 15 stat. 44.

28. Section 25, Judiciary Act of 1789, Act of Sept. 24, 1789, 1 Stat. 73.

29. Frank L. Magnum, 237 U.S. 309, 335 (1915).

30. Professor Warren's work has become the standard account, but there is an interesting challenge in Ritz, *Rewriting the History of the Judiciary Act.*

31. Erie R. Co v. Tompkins, 304 U.S. 67, 78 (1938).

32. Martha Field, "Sources of Law: The Scope of Federal Common Law," 99 *Harv. L. Rev.* 881 (1986).

33. 28 U.S.C. § 2254.

34. Joseph Hoffmann and William Stuntz, "Habeas after the Revolution," 1993 *Sup. Ct. Rev.* 65.

35. The original act was enacted in 1793. With some modifications over the years, the current version is 28 U.S.C. § 2283.

36. Younger v. Harris, 401 U.S. 37, 46 (1971).

37. The Bankruptcy Amendments and Federal Judgeship Act of 1984, Pub. L. No. 98-353, 28 U.S.C. 152.

38. See, generally, Richard Fallon, "Of Legislative Courts, Administrative Agencies, and Article III," 101 *Harv. L. Rev.* 915 (1988).

39. Michigan v. Long, 463 U.S. 1832, 1040–41 (1983).

Part II

Analysis

Four basic ideas run through the analysis of Article III. The most basic is the general principle of separation of powers, represented in the inevitable tension between an unelected judicial branch and a fundamentally democratic government. The policies of separation of powers are the fundamental explanation for Article III as a whole. This volume, however, is devoted to the specific text of section 2, which has been largely driven by three particular ideas. The first idea is the flexibility resulting from the decision not to resolve the status of courts below the Supreme Court. The second idea is the necessity to implement the structure of federalism in the day-to-day work of courts. And the third idea is the structural change made necessary by the underlying evolution from a simple common-law world to an inordinately complex global regulatory environment.

TAKING JURISDICTION WHICH IS GIVEN

The legislative history of the Constitutional Convention in Philadelphia, in part I, discusses the historical compromise that made Article III possible. Its central feature was the founders' decision to leave to a future Congress the issue whether to create any federal courts below the Supreme Court. This postponement necessarily meant that the Constitution could not define with precision what power, exactly, the lower federal courts had, if any. The general language of Article III, defining the "judicial power of the United States," sets an outer limit to what the jurisdiction of these courts would be. In broad terms, no court could decide a case unless the case presented some sort of application of federal law or involved particular parties—parties either from different states or with some special status of their own. But the compromise meant that the Constitution could not actually give jurisdiction to these lower courts, nor could it make precise how the Supreme Court's appellate jurisdiction would work, without knowing the courts from which the appeals would come.

Conversely, the developments reflected in the cases described in part I show the central importance of the idea of judicial review, of the idea that the independence of federal courts is the primary security for the integrity of government and for the protection of whatever minority might be the target du jour in Washington. Although this essential role for the federal courts was not explicit in the Constitution, it has become the most widely accepted feature of our constitutional system.

Unfortunately, these two ideas inevitably come into conflict. If Congress can restrict the jurisdiction of the federal courts, which is what the Constitution says it can do, then the courts lack the strength to deny Congress its will. But if the Courts can exert power over Congress, which is what many now think the Constitution must mean, then the actual and explicit language of Article III must be addressed.

With respect to the Supreme Court, section 2 first provides for the Supreme Court's original jurisdiction in suits between states and cases involving foreign diplomats. Then this language follows: "In all the other Cases before mentioned, the supreme Court shall have appellate Jurisdiction, both as to Law and Fact, with such Exceptions, and under such Regulations as the Congress shall make." The phrase "with such Exceptions" is the heart of the controversy about appellate jurisdiction. With respect to federal courts below the Supreme Court, section 1 begins by saying that the federal judicial power is vested in the Supreme Court "and in such inferior Courts as the Congress may from time to time ordain and establish."

The text of the Constitution does not refer at all to congressional power to limit jurisdiction of *state* courts, but well-accepted jurisdictional statutes have long barred some state court jurisdiction (in patent cases, for example) and have provided for the mandatory removal of many cases to federal courts on the request of one party. Also established in long and unquestioned historical practice, there are some disputes that the Constitution would allow to be heard in federal court but that have never in fact been within the jurisdiction of any federal court simply because no jurisdictional statute allows it. The simplest example is a suit "between Citizens of different States," included in the list of the federal judicial power in section 2. No such suit, however, can be heard in a federal court unless the statutory minimal amount in controversy ($75,000 today) is involved. Such smaller diversity cases must be tried only in a state court. Even after appeal to the state's highest court, the judicial code has no provision allowing appeal of such a diversity case to the U.S. Supreme Court. This limitation has not been a major controversy, probably because few people see the diversity jurisdiction as such an eternal verity of a free people that even a small claims diversity suit must be made federal. Where serious regional prejudice has threatened national values, the Supreme Court has been able to find some other basis of jurisdiction. During the 1960s, for example, some state courts in the South allowed large judgments for minor defamations of local segregationist officials by national media, in cases that fell outside diversity jurisdiction under the doctrine of Strawbridge v. Curtiss (1806). In the major case of New York Times v. Sullivan (1964), the U.S. Supreme Court reversed one such judgment, in the process creating a new set of substantive First Amendment rights in defamation cases. These substantive First Amendment rights provided the only basis for federal review by the Court. Without the newly minted rights, unreviewable diversity judgments by hostile state courts might have prevented national news coverage of the civil rights movement. As we see throughout this study, there is an inevitable interplay between the power to define substantive law and the question of jurisdiction.

Writing in 1984, Gerald Gunther[1] described four periods during which Congress considered substantial measures to overturn Supreme Court decisions by removing its jurisdiction. Following the Court's exercise of authority over state high courts in 1816 (Martin v. Hunter's Lessee, discussed in part I), Congress in the 1820s considered a number of attacks to take away the authority originally conferred by section 25 of the Judiciary Act of 1789. These proposals were intended to undo the nationalist vision that supports the key decisions of the Marshall Court and were early signals of the depth of state rights' resistance to the emerging constitutional order. None of these proposals passed. Following the Civil War, however, proponents of Reconstruction succeeded in passing a statute designed to prevent the Supreme Court from reviewing the imprisonment of the Reconstruction's enemies as well as its critics. The most important of these legislative acts reached the Supreme Court in *Ex parte* McCardle (1868). The *McCardle* case remains the only real authority on the question of congressional power, but, as we shall see, its ultimate ambiguity has simply added to arguments on both sides. In the 1950s, amid concern about the influence of communism, Congress considered a number of bills designed to eliminate the power of the federal courts to interfere with "national security." None of them passed. Again in the early 1980s, there were efforts to restrict judicial power over "social issues" such as school prayer and abortion. Similar legislative proposals over issues such as legislative prayers, gay marriage, and flag burning have been made in more recent decades. Since Gunther wrote, Congress passed three measures in 1996, aimed at controlling the federal courts' reviewing power over prison conditions, capital punishment, and the rights of aliens. And most recently, the Military Commissions Act of 2006 purports to deprive federal courts of jurisdiction to review the situation of prisoners at Guantanamo.

Constitutional scholars and other writers disagree not only about the detailed meaning of Article III's language on this issue. More fundamentally, they divide over the deeper policy question, a question in the end of the relationship between the independence of the judiciary and the supremacy of popular will in a democracy. Surprisingly, these divisions do not follow an easy ideological pattern. Charles Black (*Decision According to Law,* 1981) and Michael Perry (*The Courts, the Constitution, and Human Rights*, 1982), two scholars who have distinguished themselves by articulating a broad and, in general, "activist" agenda for the Supreme Court, have nonetheless argued that the legislature has nearly complete power to overturn the Supreme Court by removing its jurisdiction. In their view, the ultimate power of Congress over the Court explains why the Court itself is a democratic institution. If the Court is an essentially democratic institution, facile objections to its work as elitist must disappear.

A different, powerful constitutional tradition, however, derives cleanly from Hamilton's language in Federalist No. 78:

> [W]here the will of the legislature, declared in its statutes, stands in opposition to that of the people, declared in the Constitution, the judges ought to be governed by the latter rather than the former. They ought to regulate their decisions by the fundamental laws, rather than by those which are not fundamental.[2]

These sentiments could hardly be implemented if the legislature had the power to overturn constitutional decisions by ordinary legislation.

Relying on the language of the Constitution, even a literalist needs to consider three possible ways of reconciling the text with Hamilton's classic contrary formulation. First, within the four corners of the Exceptions Clause, two words could be used to limit the power of Congress: (1) fact and (2) exceptions.

Fact

The clause allows the Supreme Court "appellate jurisdiction, both as to Law and Fact, with such Exceptions. . . ." If "exceptions" modifies only "fact," then this provision would simply give Congress the power to protect the integrity of a jury's fact-finding verdict, a task later accomplished explicitly when the Sixth Amendment provided that "no fact tried by a jury, shall be otherwise re-examined in any Court of the United States, than according to the rules of the common law." Logically, it is perfectly possible to read these texts to mean that the Framers, in Article III, originally gave Congress the power to protect jury verdicts from the Supreme Court. The Sixth Amendment thereafter took that power out of the hands of Congress and, by self-executing language, guaranteed the integrity of the jury's findings. The main objection to this logical argument is the absence of any contemporaneous expression of it. Others also object on grounds of punctuation, that the comma after the word "fact" balances the comma beginning the parenthetical phrase ", both as to Law and Fact," making plain that the following Exceptions Clause applies both to law and fact. This observation about punctuation certainly seems strong in light of usage in the twenty-first century, but an honest observer should admit that many of the commas in the Constitution seem peculiar to the modern ear: for example, the very beginning of Article III ("The judicial Power of the United States, shall be vested. . . .").

Exceptions

The word "exceptions" connotes a minor part removed from a larger whole whose integrity is not destroyed. If I sold you my car, "except" for the drive train and body, and you ended up paying $10,000 for a radio and battery, a court might well grant you rescission. So, if Congress stripped the federal courts of the essence of their constitutional role, this would no longer be an exception. The problem here is that the argument is incomplete without a definition of what that "essential" role is, and that role cannot be defined within the bounds of Article III itself. In this sense, the "essential functions" argument is not, then, a strict textual argument.

The second way to square the text with Hamilton's vision of judicial review would be to rely on the words "all cases" as they appear at the very beginning of Article III, section 2: "The Judicial Power shall extend to all cases ... arising under this Constitution. . . ." Focusing on the word "all" would lead to the conclusion that the only way Congress could restrict the power of the Supreme Court would be to ensure that the case could at least be heard in some other federal court. Although this theory coincides with a celebrated dictum of Justice Story's in Martin v. Hunter's Lessee (1816), it generally has been rejected because Congress has in fact never vested the entire judicial power in the federal courts—the exclusion of some diversity cases, discussed earlier, is the most obvious example. Akhil Amar[3] has recently reinvigorated this argument by (1) distinguishing "cases" from "controversies" in the language of Article III; (2) pointing out that the disputes in diversity are "controversies" rather than cases; and (3) observing that the judicial power extends to "all cases," but the word "all" is omitted in references to "controversies." Amar's argument is strong in logic and the language of Article III but has not, as yet, shaped the debate—perhaps because of its novelty and perhaps because most constitutional commentators find it more persuasive to defend their positions by the substantive evocation of an essential role for the Supreme Court (i.e., that close reading of the constitutional text is not itself a favored interpretive method).

The third way to reconcile the text of Article III with Federalist No. 78 is to read the Exceptions Clause in light of the rest of the Constitution. Seen this way, the Bill of Rights, the prohibition in Article I against the suspension of habeas corpus, and Article I's Necessary and Proper Clause all constitute limits on this congressional power, just as they limit the power to regulate commerce or any other power vested in Congress. Like the "essential functions" theory, this position entails applying subtle constitutional theories beyond the language and history of Article III itself.

An interesting feature of this particular constitutional issue is that there has been an enormous scholarly interest in the subject but not even one Supreme Court case squarely addressing it. The closest that the Court has yet come is *Ex parte* McCardle in 1868. McCardle, a civilian journalist, was arrested by the Army and awaiting trial before a military court for the offense of publishing inflammatory editorials. Military jurisdiction over civilians was authorized by the Military Reconstruction Act of 1867, whose provisions were generally expected to be struck down by the Supreme Court. While McCardle's habeas corpus appeal was pending in that Court, Congress repealed the statute authorizing his appeal. The Supreme Court accordingly dismissed his appeal, in the process issuing a statement that seems at first to answer this question of congressional power definitively:

> We are not at liberty to inquire into the motives of the legislature. We can only examine into its power under the Constitution; and the power to make exceptions to the appellate jurisdiction of this court is given by express words.... Without jurisdiction the court cannot proceed at all in any cause.[4]

This passage certainly seems to validate the full reach of congressional power. Consider this modern application: If the legislature forbids Supreme Court jurisdiction in any abortion case because it disapproves of the Court's abortion rights decisions, there can be no inquiry into the legislative motive, and the Court simply loses the power to review a state court conviction. But at the very end of the opinion in *McCardle*, the Court observes that there was a different statute, still in force, under which McCardle could have independently obtained the writ of habeas corpus. An older statute, one that Congress apparently had neglected to repeal, allowed McCardle the option of filing a petition for habeas corpus in the Supreme Court, rather than docketing his case as an appeal from the denial of the writ in the trial court. So the situation could amount to no more than allowing Congress to specify the route a habeas appeal must follow—and the powerful language just quoted might not be relevant in a different case in which there were no route at all to the Supreme Court.

There was a striking reprise of *McCardle* and its ambiguity in 1996. In the Antiterrorism and Effective Death Penalty Act of 1996, Congress prohibited a successive habeas corpus petition unless a federal court of appeals first determined that the petition met certain highly restrictive criteria. The Act then prohibits a petition to the U.S. Supreme Court for the writ of certiorari if the court of appeals denies permission for the successive habeas action. Because the writ of certiorari is the basic means for appealing a lower court decision, it appeared that Congress had deprived the Supreme Court of jurisdiction to review some potential challenges under the Constitution. In assessing the potential seriousness of this limitation, it is worth remembering that the courts of appeals in recent years have been willing to declare invalid some Supreme Court decisions that the Supreme Court itself has not overruled. Thus, the Court of Appeals for the Fourth Circuit recently declared the *Miranda* decision invalid in light of a subsequent statute. Although that court of appeals decision was duly overturned by the Supreme Court (Dickerson v. United States, 2000), it illustrates the potential significance of allowing a court of appeals to block Supreme Court review. By a striking historical irony, however, when the jurisdiction-blocking provisions of the 1996 statute reached the Supreme Court, it developed that a habeas petitioner today has the same option that existed in McCardle's day, that is, the option of filing an original habeas corpus petition in the Supreme Court as another way to review a trial court judgment. The Supreme Court easily upheld the statute, observing that the jurisdiction of the Supreme Court had not been eliminated after all (Felker v. Turpin, 1996). To similarly inconclusive effect was the Court's 2006 decision in Hamdan v. Rumsfield, concerning the reach of a 2005 statute that had stripped the federal courts' jurisdiction to hear claims by any "alien detained by the Department of Defense at Guantanamo, Cuba." The Supreme Court avoided the question of jurisdiction when it found that the statute did not apply to lawsuits already pending at the time of enactment.[5]

The long historical pattern of congressional step and Supreme Court side-step seems too well practiced to be a simple oversight. Like some issues in long and lively marriages, it is hard to resist the conclusion that the parties are careful to preserve some ambiguities because these uncertainties can deflect forces that might otherwise destroy the very possibility of a continuing relationship.

ADDING JURISDICTION WHICH IS NOT GIVEN

Questions of Federal Law

The Constitution provides that the "Judicial Power shall extend to all Cases, in Law and Equity, arising under this Constitution, [and] the Laws of the United States." This clause makes clear that federal courts have jurisdiction over cases founded on the federal Constitution or statutes, often referred to as "federal questions." As Chief Justice Marshall stated in Osborn v. Bank of the United States (1824), Article III "enables the judicial department to receive jurisdiction to the full extent of the Constitution, laws, and treaties of the United States, when any question respecting them shall assume such a form that the judicial power is capable of acting on it."

A key problem is that many cases have some question about federal law in them but may actually turn on state law. A defendant in a state criminal case may object to the constitutionality of one particular search. An automobile accident may have been exacerbated by the design of an interstate highway. A soldier may have driven too fast and argued that he was privileged to do so because he was reporting for duty. The permutations are almost endless.

For the moment, let's focus on cases filed initially in a federal trial court. The situation is simpler in the case of an appeal to the U.S. Supreme Court. Once the case has been winnowed on appeal, it is easy to tell whether its outcome depends on a decision of federal law. If so, there is jurisdiction. Even here, there is the possibility of a complex problem in cases in which the state and federal law may not be truly independent of each other. That problem will be discussed later. When the suit is initially filed in a federal trial court, before the process of decision has eliminated any possibilities, it cannot be known in advance on what particular rules the outcome will finally depend.

Until 1875, there was no general statute giving federal trial courts jurisdiction to try federal questions. Strange as this lack seems to the modern eye, basically few substantive federal statutes called for enforcement in litigation. In some specific cases, Congress conferred jurisdiction to sue under particular statutes when it enacted them in the first place. Then, for the first time in the Judiciary Act of 1875, Congress granted to federal trial courts original jurisdiction of "all suits of a civil nature . . . arising under the Constitution of laws of the United States, or treaties. . . ." Although this language is barely distinguishable from that of Article III, it has long been interpreted as narrower in scope than the Constitution. That is, there are cases in which Congress could confer jurisdiction but has not done so. The same, as we shall see, is true of diversity jurisdiction.

In rough terms, a case arises under federal law in the trial court if the plaintiff alleges a right or interest that is substantially founded on federal constitutional law, federal law, federal common law, federal statutory law, treaty law, or federal regulations. The federal claim must appear as part of the plaintiff's cause of action in a well-pleaded complaint—the plaintiff cannot simply mention the existence of federal law in a garrulous complaint. If the plaintiff only presents claims based on state law, it is not enough for the defendant to plead a federal defense. Nor is it sufficient for a plaintiff to file a complaint anticipating that the defendant will raise a federal defense to present a federal question. Nor will it suffice if the defendant claims by way of reply to a state lawsuit that the plaintiff, in turn, owes the defendant something because of federal law. To present a federal question, the plaintiff must begin by stating a claim in which a federal element is essential to the cause of action. If a plaintiff files a complaint containing both state and federal law claims, then the federal court has the discretion to exercise jurisdiction, based on whether the claims derive from a "common nucleus of operative fact" and are so related or intertwined that it is practical to try them together. For the most part then, the existence of federal trial court jurisdiction has become a question about the interpretation of the jurisdictional statutes rather than of Article III. The constitutional question that lurks portentously in the background is what might be the outer limit on congressional power to relax these general rules. This problem is usually called "protective jurisdiction."

Protective Jurisdiction

If there is no federal question presented in the plaintiff's complaint, may Congress nevertheless authorize federal jurisdiction beyond the subjects listed in Article III of the Constitution? Does Article III limit the jurisdiction that federal courts can be granted, or can Congress confer federal jurisdiction whenever it is "necessary and proper," using the language of congressional power generally? And even if federal courts are limited to Article III cases, how broad is the meaning of "arising under" the laws of the United States?

On several occasions, Congress has given federal courts jurisdiction over state law claims that do not involve federal questions or diversity of citizenship. The theory of this protective jurisdiction is that when a subject lies within the reach of the legislative powers of Congress under Article I of the Constitution, Congress may enact a statute granting federal jurisdiction over the cases involving that subject, even if the underlying substantive claims are predicated on state law, not federal law.[6] This argument is even stronger when Congress had already granted some federal rights or has articulated a federal policy in a particular area of law. There may be several different reasons why Congress may choose to create a federal forum for claims involving state law. Congress may grant federal jurisdiction over state law claims to prevent state courts, which have diverse laws, from interfering with a federal policy.[7] Or, Congress may find that the neutrality of state courts is suspect or that the procedures of some state courts are inadequate.

The concept of protective jurisdiction begins with Osborn v. Bank of the United States, which arose as a result of the decision by Congress to charter the second Bank of the United States in 1816. The Supreme Court had held in McCulloch v. Maryland (1819) that Congress had the authority to establish a national bank and that states did not have the power to tax it. But that decision did not deter the state of Ohio from assessing a $50,000 annual tax on each office of the Bank of the United States. Defying a federal court injunction, the state auditor, Ralph Osborn, broke into the bank and took more than $100,000, giving most of it to the state treasurer. When the federal court ordered Osborn to return the money, he refused and appealed to the Supreme Court, claiming that the federal court did not have jurisdiction.

At issue in this case was the federal statutory provision that the Bank of the United States could "sue and be sued, and defend and be defended in any of the state courts having competent jurisdiction, and any federal circuit court of the United States." Writing for the Court, Chief Justice Marshall held that the federal statute established jurisdiction in the federal circuit courts over *all* suits involving the Bank of the United States, because every case brought by or against the bank would involve multiple federal questions. Marshall concluded that the "arising under" language of Article III authorized extending jurisdiction to the federal courts over all suits brought by or against the congressionally chartered bank, even if a suit was based entirely on *state law*. The Court did not, in other words, require that the case itself raise any federal issues at all, although of course this particular lawsuit did. There would have been jurisdiction under the language of the statute even if Ralph Osborn had been a private citizen simply suing to collect a private debt. Nor did the Court even allude to the likelihood that the Ohio state courts might have been prejudiced in favor of their own official collecting tax money, although that too might well have been the case.

The Court instead relied on the broadest possible argument. To sue, the Bank must necessarily refer to the law that gives it the authority to sue, which in this case is the law that gives the federal courts jurisdiction. The defendant might challenge the validity of this law, which is a federal law. The theoretical possibility accordingly exists that there would be a dispute about federal law, which is enough to warrant a federal trial. In effect, then, a case arises under a law that gives jurisdiction, which is to say that a law giving jurisdiction automatically, or perhaps "tautologically," satisfies the "arising under" requirement. Given the breadth of this reasoning, the only limit on Article III jurisdiction would be Congress's power to legislate in the first place—limits given in Article I not Article III.

If *Osborn* stood alone, the answer to this question would be that Article III, section 2, places no limits on congressional power. For more than a century, the occasion to reevaluate Marshall's decision did not arise. For one thing, Congress had no reason to enact laws specifically conferring jurisdiction in particular classes of cases once the Judiciary Act conferred general federal question jurisdiction. If the facts of the *Osborn* case happened after 1875, the case would have been within the general statute because the gravamen was that the actions of Osborn directly violated a federal substantive law. Two significant cases in the twentieth century led the Court to revisit the issue.

Lincoln Mills

The federal labor laws that began with the New Deal devoted much effort to the process of creating a collective bargaining contract. They did not, however, trouble to specify the law that should be applied to the interpretation and enforcement of these contracts once they were actually formed. An ample body of state contract law already existed in every state. Textile Workers v. Lincoln Mills of Alabama (1957) involved a provision that suits for violation of contracts between an employer and a labor organization could be brought in federal court without regard to diversity of citizenship.[8] Here, a collective bargaining agreement provided that there would be no strikes or work stoppages, and that grievances would be heard by an arbitrator after certain procedures were followed. When the union filed grievances and followed all the required procedural steps, it requested arbitration according to the terms of the contract. When the employer refused to go through arbitration, the union filed suit in federal court in accordance with the federal statute.

The U.S. district court ordered the employer to comply with the contract, but the court of appeals reversed, holding that the district court had no authority under either state or federal law to grant this relief.[9] The issue before the Supreme Court was whether the district court had jurisdiction and, if so, whether it could grant relief under state or federal law. Justice Douglas, writing for the Court, held that the federal court had jurisdiction because federal substantive law would apply when interpreting and enforcing the statute, not state law. Although the statute itself did not specify any details in which federal courts would interpret the contracts and enforce them, the Court concluded that federal courts could fashion "federal common law." As a substantive matter, the decision that federal courts should fashion from scratch a federal common law of contracts is almost stunning in its novelty and audacity. The only plausible reason to impose this creative task on the courts was surely the Court's concern that, otherwise, there would be no federal jurisdiction unless the full reach of the *Osborn* case was reaffirmed.

Justice Frankfurter dissented vigorously. He noted that the majority's decision could bring into conflict state law and federal law, and state courts and federal courts. He argued that the contract remedy should be based on state law, which traditionally has governed the law of contracts. He criticized the majority's use of federal common law, stating that "[t]here are severe limits on judicial inventiveness even for the most imaginative judges. The law is not a 'brooding omnipresence in the sky,' and it cannot be drawn from there like nitrogen from the air." Because Frankfurter concluded that state law should apply, he then took on the issue of whether Congress could ever grant "protective jurisdiction" when there is no diversity of citizenship and when the legal claims presented were based on state law.

Justice Frankfurter's position was that "[p]rotective jurisdiction . . . cannot be justified under any view of the allowable scope to be given to Article III." He responded to a series of arguments condoning protective jurisdiction. First, some argued that if Congress *could* constitutionally grant federal rights in a particular area of law, then Congress could also provide a federal forum for parties to litigate, even if Congress decided not to grant those federal rights.[10] Frankfurter responded, "the truly technical restrictions of Article III are not met or respected by a beguiling phrase that the greater power here must include the lesser . . . it is obvious that very different considerations apply to cases involving questions of federal law and those turning solely on state law." He then took on Professor Mishkin's argument[11] that, when Congress has an articulated and active federal policy regulating a field, the "arising under" clause of Article III permits giving federal courts *all* cases in the area, including those substantively governed by state law. Justice Frankfurter rejected this theory, although less brusquely than the first, on the ground that there must be, at an absolute minimum, some federal legal question potentially at issue.

Frankfurter acknowledged that there were "exceptional cases" in which the Court had found federal jurisdiction was present, although there was no diversity of citizenship and the resolution of the plaintiff's claim probably would be governed by state law.[12] But Frankfurter argued that "[a]t least in *Osborn* and the bankruptcy cases, a substantive federal law was present somewhere in the background." He also distinguished *Osborn* by stating that "the historical setting was vastly different, and the juristic entity was completely the creature of federal law, one engaged in carrying out essential governmental functions."

Even if *Osborn* did have some "analytic similarity" to the present case, Frankfurter argued it should not be extended, because federal jurisdiction was found in that case because a federal question *could* arise, which is not the usual criterion upon which federal jurisdiction can be granted. Frankfurter thought that if a federal question did not clearly present itself, the case should be resolved by state courts in accordance with state law. And if a federal question did in fact eventually arise, removal procedures would provide federal courts jurisdiction over the case. Justice Frankfurter concluded that Congress could not empower federal courts to enforce labor contracts unless it specified that federal law governed them, thus making explicit the exact argument that the majority opinion avoided by finding a congressional mandate to create a federal common law of contracts.

Justice Frankfurter's basic proposition has its roots in the famous case of Marbury v. Madison (1803). In this case, President John Adams had appointed William Marbury to fill a vacancy on the Court but failed to deliver his commission before leaving office. Marbury sued under a law passed by Congress, which authorized the Court to issue a writ of mandamus, to compel Secretary of State James Madison (under President Jefferson) to deliver his commission. Writing for the Court, Justice Marshall held that Congress could not authorize the Court to issue a writ of mandamus because the Court did not have jurisdiction in Article III. Marshall reasoned that if Congress could grant further powers to the Court beyond those listed in Article III, then the enumeration of powers in the Constitution would be pointless. Although *Marbury* is mainly remembered for its broader holding that the federal courts may disregard statutes they find to be unconstitutional, its narrower holding is that the granting of jurisdiction in some categories excludes jurisdiction in all others.

Tidewater

The issue whether Article III's grants of jurisdiction are exclusive had divided the Court inconclusively in National Mutual Insurance Co. v. Tidewater Transfer Co., Inc. (1949). The plaintiff, who was a citizen of the District of Columbia, sued another citizen who was domiciled in Virginia over an insurance contract. The Supreme Court held in 1804 that citizens of the District of Columbia were not citizens of a state and, therefore, could not sue or be sued in diversity cases.[13] In 1940, however, Congress authorized federal jurisdiction over suits between citizens of the District of Columbia and citizens of the different states. The district court held that, although jurisdictional requirements were met by the act of Congress, the law did not comply with the Constitution.[14] The Supreme Court's decision found five votes to uphold the statute, but these five justices did not agree on the theory of that conclusion.

Justice Jackson, writing for himself and two other justices (Justices Black and Burton), argued that Congress could not grant federal courts jurisdiction under Article III, because the District of Columbia is not a state within Article III. So there was no diversity of citizenship, nor was there a federal question, because the suit involved a contract dispute governed by local law. Justice Jackson reasoned that "cases between citizens of the District of Columbia and those of the states were not included in the catalogue of controversies over which the Congress could give jurisdiction to the federal courts by virtue of Article III."

Justice Jackson argued, however, that Congress could grant federal courts jurisdiction through its Article I powers. "Article I empowers Congress to exercise exclusive legislation over the District of Columbia, and also to make all Laws which shall be necessary and proper for carrying into 'Execution' such powers." Justice Jackson gave examples of the Court upholding congressional authorization of jurisdiction pursuant to Article I, including that establishment of the Court of Claims,[15] the authorization of district courts to sit as courts of claims, and the delegation of district courts to handle bankruptcy cases. The justices contended that Article III could not be the source of power under these types of cases, because there was no diversity and no federal law question. The three justices concluded that in this case, because Congress had relied on powers in Article I, the grant of federal court jurisdiction was constitutional. The three justices also acknowledged that there are limits to Congress's reliance on Article I jurisdiction: "Of course there are limits to the nature of duties which Congress may impose on the constitutional courts vested with the federal judicial power. The doctrine of the separation of power is fundamental to our system."

Two justices (Justices Rutledge and Murphy) concurred in the judgment upholding the statute, but they argued that Congress could not expand jurisdiction beyond the powers enumerated in Article III. "I do not think we or Congress can override the limits [of Article III] through the invocation of Article I without making the Constitution a self-contradictory instrument." They concluded, however, that the very special nature of the District of Columbia allowed this particular statute to stand.

Four justices (Chief Justice Vinson and Justices Douglas, Frankfurter, and Reed) dissented. They joined the two concurrences in rejecting the theory that Article I's legislative powers alone would justify adding to the jurisdiction of federal courts but disagreed with the concurrences in finding special status for the District of Columbia. In all, then, there were a total of six votes agreeing that Congress could not expand jurisdiction beyond Article III of the Constitution, reaffirming the broad rule of Marbury v. Madison. Nonetheless, there have been exceptional cases in which the Court has held that there is federal court jurisdiction, even though the power exceeds certain functions set out in Article III. For example, the Court has held that the Court of Claims and the Court of Customs, which are Article III federal courts, could be assigned additional functions beyond deciding cases and controversies.[16] The Court has also held it permissible for Congress to assign the Court of Appeals for the District of Columbia administrative tasks not specifically found in Article III.[17] In short, the Court has not succeeded in reconciling the implications of two great decisions of Chief Justice Marshall—the expansive reading of *Osborn* and the restrictive implications of *Marbury*.

Verlinden

As was true with the pragmatic result in *Tidewater* (it does, after all, make good common sense that residents of the District of Columbia are subject to the same out-of-state prejudices as residents of the several states) it seems that cogent federal interests may outweigh purely theoretical sensibilities concerning the scope of Article III. In Verlinden B.V. v. Central Bank of Nigeria (1983), the Republic of Nigeria entered into a contract with Verlinden, a Dutch corporation for the delivery of cement. The contract provided that Nigeria was to establish a letter of credit from a Bank in Amsterdam and that the contract would be governed by the laws of the Netherlands, with disputes being resolved before the International Chamber of Commerce in Paris. Verlinden filed a complaint contending that the bank of Nigeria improperly obtained a letter of credit from a firm in New York. They sued in a U.S. district court pursuant to a federal statute providing that district courts shall have original jurisdiction without regard to the amount in controversy of any nonjury civil action against a foreign state "with respect to which the foreign state is not entitled to immunity."[18] Although the Bank of Nigeria argued that it was immune from suit, which is a federal defense, the plaintiff's substantive rights were not based on any federal law.

The district court held that Article III extends to suits by foreign corporations against foreign sovereigns, because there would be an essential federal element in all suits brought against foreign states. But it dismissed the suit, finding the defendant was immune. The court of appeals affirmed the dismissal, but on different grounds, holding the Act exceeded the scope of Article III of the Constitution. It argued that actions by foreign plaintiffs against foreign sovereigns presented no federal question, because the plaintiff's complaint was not based on federal law. The only federal issue was Nigeria's defense of immunity. The court of appeals also concluded there was no jurisdiction under the diversity or alienage clauses of Article III, which do not mention suits between two aliens.

A unanimous Supreme Court reversed, upholding the statute under the heading of "arising under" federal law—an appropriate basis, they thought, for the statutory grant of federal jurisdiction in actions brought by a foreign plaintiff against foreign sovereigns. The Court drew support from *Osborn*, saying that it "reflects a broad conception of 'arising under' jurisdiction, according to which Congress may confer on the federal courts jurisdiction over any case or controversy that *might* call for the application of federal law." Even so, the Court declined to define the breadth of that decision, observing that it "need not resolve the precise boundaries of Article III jurisdiction, however, since the present case does not involve mere speculative possibility that a federal question may arise at some point in the proceeding."

The Court held that "a suit against a foreign state under this Act necessarily raises questions of substantive federal law at the very outset, and hence clearly 'arises under' federal law, as that term is used in Article III." The Court reasoned that because Congress had authority over foreign commerce and foreign relations in Article I, Congress also had the power to decide as a matter of federal law whether foreign nations could be sued in federal courts.

> The act codifies the standards governing foreign sovereign immunity as an aspect of substantive federal law ... Congress deliberately sought to channel cases against foreign sovereigns away from the state courts and into federal courts, thereby reducing the potential for a multiplicity of conflicting results among the courts of the 50 states.[19]

The Court noted in footnote 17 of *Verlinden* that "[i]n view of our conclusion that proper actions by foreign plaintiffs under the [Act] are within Art. III 'arising under' jurisdiction, we need not consider ... [if] the Act is constitutional as an aspect of so-called 'protective jurisdiction.'" So, in a technical sense, the Court has not yet resolved the theoretical question of protective jurisdiction. That issue would have been presented squarely if the defendant had not raised the defense of sovereign immunity. There are powerful reasons that a federal court, rather than a state court, should hear disputes like this one. State courts are singularly ill-equipped to decide questions involving foreign governments. Yet the fact that most foreign sovereigns have assets and do business in the United States makes an American court of some kind (state or federal) an increasingly likely forum in which to hear the case when they are sued by another foreign entity. In a case taken seriously by the foreign government, federal interests abroad may well be at risk of reprisal, and both diplomatic and military interests may be compromised. No sensible institutional arrangement would leave national interests at the mercy of state court judgments in such cases. This general problem was, as we read in part I, a source of specific dissatisfaction with the Articles of Confederation. The Supreme Court in *Verlinden* seemed to acknowledge as much when it wrote of "the potential for a multiplicity of conflicting results among the courts of the 50 states."

So it seems difficult to resist the conclusion that overriding federal interests have always prevailed over the niceties of Article III. Protecting the Bank of the United States from a rapacious state treasury, a labor contract from the politics of a state's courts, residents "inside the Beltway" from state juries, and foreign governments from the general shortcomings of state judges in international economic affairs all have found their way to federal court. But it is still true that each of these decisions could be upheld on an alternative basis, however strained.

It would probably be a fair summary of the situation to suggest that a law that squarely challenged the issue in a matter of obvious national interest would be upheld. A good example would be the Price-Anderson Act, which provides the following:

> With respect to any public liability action arising out of or resulting from a nuclear incident, the United States district court . . . shall have original jurisdiction without regard to the citizenship of any party or the amount in controversy.
>
> [T]he substantive rules for decision in such action shall be derived from the law of the State in which the nuclear incident involved occurs, unless such a law is inconsistent with the provisions of such section.[20]

The national ramifications of any different policy toward nuclear energy would effectively cripple the ability of Congress to set national policy. But it is doubtful that the actual logic of such a holding would also be applied to a more obviously politicized measure, say to a federal statute that limited punitive damages to $100,000 in medical malpractice cases and then gave all malpractice cases to federal courts on the theory that there might be an issue with the punitive damages cap.

THE BOUNDARIES OF A CASE (OR CONTROVERSY)

In English common law, when the Constitution was adopted, it was quite clear what a "case" was. It was a lawsuit defined by the forms of action at common law, falling within a prescribed or known formula. Thus, each case proceeded by fitting it into a known template, allowing a particular remedy for a specified wrong. A typical example of this process would be Marbury's suit in mandamus. Mandamus was a writ, issued against an official, ordering the official to perform a nondiscretionary duty, in this case, ordering Madison to deliver Marbury's personal property, a certain now-famous commission. If the facts at trial had revealed a different wrong, say that Madison had destroyed the commission, Marbury's suit would have had to be dismissed. Thus, in applying the language of Article III to determine the existence of jurisdiction, it would have been clear who the parties were and what, exactly, the issue was. Procedure in civil actions no longer follows this system of fitting new cases within predefined templates. Parties can be added as necessary to do justice, remedies can be modified, and new substantive theories can be implemented from case to case. As a result, it is hard to say what a "case" might turn out to be or who the parties really are. The fluidity of defining a case has greatly complicated the question of what Article III gives courts the power to do.

Standing

The simple idea of standing is that the party raising an issue must have some personal stake in its outcome. The do-gooder who perceives from a blog an outrage about to be perpetrated by the National Security Agency and sues to defend the Constitution has not stated a case because he or she lacks standing. The law of standing, at least by name, has been a creation of the twentieth century. Increased recognition of constitutional rights, development of the class action lawsuit, and judicial protection of racial equality contributed to the increased demand on the courts to resolve disputes with the government. Standing emerged largely because of the efforts of Justices Brandeis and Frankfurter. As an ideological or political matter, they supported the emerging modern legal order, which consisted particularly of an administrative state no longer defined exclusively by private law concepts such as property and contract. Litigation was no longer a vehicle for resolving disputes only between private parties; rather, litigation had become a way of restricting the power of the government to intervene in the private economic sphere. The law of standing then became a means of protecting the government's new model from judicial boundaries defined in common law terms.

Allen v. Wright

Although the Court has fluctuated in its pronouncements of standing, it seems now to have settled on a vocabulary derived from Allen v. Wright

(1984). In *Allen*, the Court held that the constitutional component of standing required a plaintiff to show "personal injury fairly traceable to the defendant's allegedly unlawful conduct and likely to be redressed by the requested relief." This statement reveals the three constitutional components of standing: personal injury, traceability of the plaintiff's injury to the defendant's allegedly unlawful conduct, and redressability. The Court concedes that these concepts are not capable of precise definition, noting that the personal injury must be "distinct and palpable, and not abstract or conjectural or hypothetical." Likewise, the injury must be "fairly" traceable to the defendant's alleged conduct, and the relief from the injury must be "likely" if a judgment is rendered favorable to the plaintiff.

In *Allen*, the class action plaintiffs were parents of black public school children. These parents alleged that the Internal Revenue Service (IRS) had not sufficiently adopted standards and procedures to deny (pursuant to the Court's ruling in Bob Jones University v. United States)[21] tax-exempt status to racially discriminatory private schools. The plaintiffs claimed that they were personally harmed by this governmental failure to act in two ways: (1) the conduct constituted federal financial support for racial segregation in education; and (2) the conduct interfered with the efforts of the federal courts and other authorities attempting to desegregate educational systems. These parents claimed that the first harm was directly traceable to the tax agency's conduct and the second harm was traceable to the agency because its conduct created incentive-orientated tax deductions that encouraged such discriminatory behavior. As relief, the plaintiffs requested a declaratory judgment against the IRS's practices and a court order requiring the IRS to deny tax exemptions to a broad class of private schools.

The Court held that the *Allen* plaintiffs lacked standing to seek a declaratory judgment against the government. The Court concluded that the plaintiffs' first alleged injury—that the IRS's conduct constituted federal financial support for racial segregation in education—was not judicially cognizable under two interpretations. First, the injury could be interpreted as a claim to have the government avoid violation of the law. However, the assertion of a right to have the government act in accordance with the law is not sufficient by itself to confer federal jurisdiction. This "right" is an abstraction rather than any particular legal claim of an individual plaintiff. Second, the plaintiffs' first alleged injury could be interpreted as a claim of stigmatizing injury caused by racial discrimination. Although the Court did not deny the severity of such noneconomic injuries, such injuries can be a basis for standing "only to those persons who are personally denied equal treatment by the challenged discriminatory conduct." Extending standing to all stigmatizing circumstances "would transform the federal courts into no more than a vehicle for the vindication of the value interests of concerned bystanders. Constitutional limits on the role of the federal courts preclude such a transformation."

The Court held that the plaintiffs' second injury was not fairly traceable to the allegedly unlawful conduct of the IRS. The *Allen* plaintiffs' second claim alleged that the conduct of the IRS interfered with the efforts of the federal courts and other authorities that have attempted to desegregate education and its social context. The Court recognized that this claim met the personal injury requirement because of the diminished ability of the plaintiffs' children to receive an education in a racially integrated school. This injury is more personal than the abstract stigmatizing injury the Court addressed in the *Allen* plaintiffs' first claim. Despite the personal injury, however, the line of causation between the government's alleged misconduct and the plaintiffs' injury was found to be attenuated because of the necessary intervention of numerous third parties, namely, the independent private schools and the parents of children attending such schools. It was uncertain whether the withdrawal of the tax-exempt status would lead to any particular school actually changing its policies, and it was just as speculative whether any parents of the students at these private schools would react to the withdrawal of tax-exempt status by enrolling their children in public schools instead. As the Court summarizes the point, these "independent decisions may not collectively have a significant effect on the ability of public-school students to receive a desegregated education."

The *Allen* Court's standing doctrine reasoning also involved an underlying separation of powers argument. Had the Court found the *Allen* plaintiffs' allegations fairly traceable to the IRS, the Court concluded, anyone could generally challenge the way in which particular governmental agencies carried out their legal obligations. These types of suits are inappropriate for federal court adjudication, as the federal courts would have to act as continuous virtual monitors "of the wisdom and soundness of Executive action,"[22] a role for which Congress is better suited. Because "the Government has traditionally been granted the widest latitude in the dispatch of its own internal affairs," federal lawsuits brought "not to enforce specific legal obligations whose violation works a direct harm, but to seek a restructuring of the apparatus established by the Executive Branch to fulfill its legal duties" cannot be supported under Article III.[23] This separation of powers argument recalls the foundational concerns of Justices Brandeis and Frankfurter.

Lujan

Another case that aided in the development of the three-part constitutional standard was Lujan v. Defenders of Wildlife (1992). In *Lujan*, the Court detailed the "irreducible constitutional minimum" of standing. The first requirement—the personal injury or "injury in fact"—was described as "an invasion of a legally-protected interest which is (a) concrete and particularized and (b) actual or imminent, not conjectural or hypothetical." The traceability requirement was specified as not the result of independent action of a third party not before the Court, and the Court noted that redressability must be likely, rather than "merely speculative."

The *Lujan* Court also addressed two issues that the *Allen* Court did not address. First, the *Lujan* Court noted that the party invoking federal jurisdiction bears the burden of establishing the elements of standing. According to the Court, a plaintiff in an old-fashioned common law claim is directly "an object of the action" and " ... ordinarily [has] little question that the action or inaction has caused him injury, and that a judgment preventing or requiring the action will redress it." However, when the plaintiffs instead allege harm based on the government's regulation of, or failure to regulate, a third party (as was the case in *Allen* and *Lujan*), the burden of proof is dramatically increased.

Second, the facts of *Lujan* required the Court to address a "citizen suit" argument. In *Lujan*, the plaintiffs alleged that they had suffered a "procedural injury" under the Endangered Species Act of 1973.[24] According to section 1540(g) of that act, "any person may commence a civil suit on his own behalf (A) to enjoin any person, including the United States and any other governmental instrumentality or agency ... who is alleged to be in violation of any provision of this chapter." The *Lujan* Court struck down this portion of the statute as unconstitutional when exercised against the government, reaffirming its position that a generally available grievance against the government "does not state an Article III case or controversy." Rather, "the ... injury required by Article III may exist solely by virtue of statutes creating legal rights, the invasion of which creates standing." Congress cannot defeat this constitutional requirement by the passing of a statute.

In developing its reasoning regarding the unavailability of citizen suits against the government, the Court noted its proper institutional role in the structure of a separated government. The Court, citing Marbury v. Madison, noted that its province "is, solely, to decide the rights of individuals," whereas "[v]indicating the *public* interest ... is the function of Congress and the chief executive." The Court's holding with respect to citizen suits had a broad impact on the congressional regulatory structure.[25] Congress had allowed for such suits as a check on what it perceived to be a failure on the part of the executive branch to properly enforce the laws in specific administrative areas, most notably (as with *Lujan*) in connection with the environment. The Court's authority for its decision seems questionable[26] and is not consistent with preexisting cases the Court used in support, which primarily suggest that standing is absent whenever there is no supporting positive law. This position seems at odds with denying standing in positively expressed citizen suits, such as in *Lujan*, as well as the Court's early rationale that "the ... injury required by Article III may exist solely by virtue of statutes creating legal rights, the invasion of which creates standing."[27] The general denial of congressionally authorized citizen suits also excludes Congress from participation in defining legal rights in ways unknown to the common law, a strange and troubling result given that the power to make the law belongs to Congress.

Constitutional requirements aside, the Court has also developed "prudential" requirements for standing that must be met by litigants. Generally speaking, these concerns are subject to congressional override—unlike the issues raised in *Lujan* or other constitutional decisions. The most significant prudential requirements note that the plaintiff's injury must be arguably within the zone of interests protected or regulated by the statutory or constitutional provision at issue and that a party cannot have standing to litigate the rights of another.[28] Ultimately, the prudential requirements may be an indication that standing is largely a matter of congressional conferral of a specific cause of action.

The "zone of interests" requirement derives from Data Processing Services Organizations v. Camp (1970), in which the Court held that the Administrative Procedure Act[29]—not Article III—required plaintiffs to have suffered an injury in fact. In the course of reaching this holding, the Court said that a plaintiff must show that he or she is "arguably within the zone of interests" protected or regulated by the statutory scheme. As applied to constitutional challenges, the zone of interests test requires the plaintiff to be an intended beneficiary of the constitutional provision at issue. Before Allen v. Wright, it had seemed that *Data Processing* might become the central case in the Court's analysis of the theoretical concept underlying standing, but that has not proven to be the case. To date, this requirement has resulted in a denial of standing only once, in Air Courier Conference v. APWU (1991). In that case, employees of the U.S. Postal Service brought suit challenging the postal service's decision to voluntarily relinquish its statutorily granted monopoly of the mails. The Court held that the employees lacked standing because they were not within the zone of interests of the statutes that created the national postal monopoly.

The second prudential standing rule, third-party standing, is closely related to the constitutional requirement of personal injury, or injury in fact. That is, a plaintiff may only litigate on the basis of injury to himself or herself. Whether third parties decide to litigate their own rights is their decision to make. However, this prudential requirement is subject to several exceptions. Generally, whether third-party standing arises is a factual inquiry, with refusal being most likely in situations in which the injury to the third party is imaginary or conjectural. In some cases, most notably Craig v. Boren (1976), the Court has allowed third-party standing when the rights of the third parties were likely to be diluted or adversely affected should a constitutional challenge to statutory authority fail.

Several Supreme Court cases have looked to the ability of the third party to raise his or her own rights in determining the permissibility of a particular litigant's standing. For example, in Barrows v. Jackson (1953), Los Angeles landowners had entered into racially restrictive covenants on land in their neighborhood. A fellow landowner permitted occupancy of her property by non-Caucasians, prompting a lawsuit by the other landowners who sought to enforce the covenant. Notably, the lawsuit was brought against the white landowner, not the nonwhite residents. The landowner raised in defense the rights of the nonwhite residents.[30] The Court allowed the third-party standing, stating "it would be difficult if not impossible for the persons whose rights are asserted to present their grievance before any court."

Third-party standing also raises questions of relationship between the third party and the litigant asserting that third party's rights. In Singleton v. Wulff (1976), a plurality of the Court believed the relationship to be significant. *Singleton* involved a doctor-patient relationship, which previously had been allowed for purposes of third-party standing, albeit without significant discussion. Schools also have been allowed to raise the constitutional rights of their students and their students' parents.[31] More recently, in Elk Grove Unified School District v. Newdow (2004), the Court held that a student cannot be represented by a parent in an action against that student's school when state law has granted the nonlitigating parent sole legal custody of the child-student and the nonlitigating parent opposes the litigating parent's representation of the child-student.

It is evident that the concepts used to define standing are malleable and unlikely to define sharply the role of the courts. It should not be surprising that the actual outcome has more to do with the Supreme Court's perception of the degree to which the courts should be creatively involved in fashioning the legal regime. This sort of self-conscious institutional reflection has resulted in a large body of decisional law that seems totally disconnected from the language of the Constitution. *Lujan* is especially ironic in this regard, because it strikes down a congressionally mandated procedure designed expressly for the purpose of using federal courts to supervise the application of a statute to government procedures.

Collateral State Law Issues

Federal courts may hear cases that involve federal questions or are within diversity jurisdiction. But federal courts may also exercise jurisdiction over state law claims if they are included in the "case." Thus, the definition of "case" becomes an important measure of constitutional jurisdiction. The scope of that concept was simple under a common-law writ in the eighteenth century, but it can be nearly amorphous in a modern class action or in a multiparty mass tort case. The first major case stating the principle was Freeman v. Howe (1860). In this case, the plaintiff filed a lawsuit in federal court against a railroad company. The federal court then authorized a federal official to seize several railroad cars to hold as security in case the plaintiff won a judgment. Later, third-party lenders (mortgagees) of the railroad company, who were not involved in the original federal suit, obtained a state court order authorizing a county sheriff to take back the cars and hold them as security for the lenders. On appeal, the U.S. Supreme Court considered two alternatives: it could allow (1) the state court to interfere with the property already before the federal court, or (2) the mortgagees to pursue their state law claims in federal court. The Court held that the third-party mortgagees could intervene and present their claims in federal court, although there was no separate basis for federal jurisdiction.

The *Freeman* case provides the foundation for the doctrine of ancillary jurisdiction. Under this doctrine, federal courts are allowed to hear claims that arise from the same set of facts, even if some of those claims do not provide a separate basis for federal jurisdiction. For example, a federal court can rule on a defendant's counterclaim based on state law, if the counterclaim arose from the same set of facts as the plaintiff's federal claims.[32] Pendent jurisdiction is a particular type of ancillary jurisdiction. A federal court exercises pendent jurisdiction when a plaintiff presents both federal and state law claims in his or her complaint, which arises out of the same set of facts, while ancillary jurisdiction includes claims that are asserted after the filing of the original complaint.[33] The first major case involving pendent jurisdiction was Siler v. Louisville & Nashville Railroad (1909), in which a railroad company sued in federal court, alleging that a state regulation fixing railroad rates violated state law and the U.S. Constitution. The state law claim did not involve a federal question or have diversity of citizenship. Nevertheless, the Supreme Court held that a federal court could adjudicate the state law claim, because the claim arose from the same facts as a federal question. This would be the case even if the plaintiff lost on the federal claim and only the state law claim remained before the federal court. In the years following *Siler*, the Court had considerable difficulty articulating the exact relationship required for the exercise of pendent jurisdiction, struggling to apply a metaphysical analysis of whether there were separate "causes of action."[34]

The test for pendent jurisdiction was articulated more pragmatically in United Mine Workers v. Gibbs (1966).[35] There, the court stated that pendent jurisdiction exists whenever there is a claim arising under federal law and the relationship between that claim and the state law claim permits the conclusion that the entire action before the federal court "comprises but one constitutional case." The federal claim must have sufficient substance to confer subject matter jurisdiction on the court and the state, and federal claims must derive from a common nucleus of operative fact. In other words, pendent jurisdiction may be exercised when there is a federal claim properly before a federal court, and a state law claim arises from the same set of facts. According to *Gibbs*, pendent jurisdiction is a matter of discretion for the trial court. Even if the federal claim is dismissed before trial for some reason, the trial court has the *power* to continue with the case, although it might more often show sound discretion to decline to exercise that power. "[P]endent jurisdiction is a doctrine of discretion, not of plaintiff's right. Its justification lies in consideration of judicial economy, convenience, and fairness to litigants; if these are not present a federal court should hesitate to exercise jurisdiction over state claims."[36] It is this practical rather than metaphysical application of the doctrine that has made it at once clearer and more useful.

In 1990, Congress codified pendent and ancillary jurisdiction under the name of "supplemental" jurisdiction.[37] This statute had as an immediate goal the overruling of Finley v. United States, a closely divided Supreme Court decision that held "pendent party" jurisdiction was not permissible unless there is a specific statutory grant. The current statute permits federal courts to hear claims against additional parties if those claims arise out of the same set of facts, even if it would not otherwise have jurisdiction. For example, if a plaintiff presents one federal claim against one defendant, and a separate state claim against a different defendant arising out of the same set of previous facts, a federal court may hear both claims in the same proceeding. The statute provides:

> [I]n any action of which the district courts have original jurisdiction, the district courts shall have supplemental jurisdiction over all other claims that are so related to claims in the action within such original jurisdiction that they form part of the same case or controversy under Article III of the United States Constitution. Such supplemental jurisdiction shall include claims that involve the joinder or intervention of additional parties.[38]

Although the Court has stated that this section essentially codifies the principles of ancillary and pendent jurisdiction laid down in *Gibbs* and other cases decided before it,[39] the statute is unclear and confusing in several particulars. It seems to change the basic structure of *Gibbs* by making supplemental jurisdiction mandatory rather than discretionary. It is unclear whether it means to nullify some well-settled details of case law. For example, under prior case law, compulsory counterclaims come within ancillary jurisdiction, but permissive counterclaims do not. It is unclear whether this distinction continues. The statute explicitly deals with certain federal procedural rules in which supplemental jurisdiction may not be exercised, such as rules 14, 19, 20, and 24; however, it does not deal with whether it can be exercised in relation to other significant rules, such as rule 13 (dealing with counterclaims) and rule 23 (dealing with diversity cases not satisfying the jurisdictional amount). The statute is explicit that federal courts do not have jurisdiction over counterclaims presented by a plaintiff against a third-party defendant, but it does not expressly disallow jurisdiction over claims presented by a third-party defendant over a nondiverse plaintiff.[40] In a serious ambiguity, the Act grants federal courts discretion whether to invoke supplemental jurisdiction over certain cases.[41] It does not specify, however, whether the entire case or only state law claims are to be remanded to state courts when supplemental jurisdiction is not exercised. Despite these flaws, the net effect of the statute seems positive. It obviates the confusing distinctions between ancillary and pendent jurisdiction, codifies preexisting case law, and simplifies many of the criteria that federal courts should use in deciding whether to exercise jurisdiction.

SECTION 2 AS A STRUCTURE OF FEDERALISM

The scheme envisioned in Article III, section 2, allowed for two possibilities. One would be that all trial courts would be state courts and the federal judicial branch would consist of but one court to review them all. Even here, no doubt, there would have been a federal admiralty court as a practical matter. This system seems impossible to imagine as the economy and its federal regulation have grown. Had things worked out that way, state courts themselves would no doubt be different in background, prestige, and structure. This model was rejected in practice from the beginning by Congress, and instead a tradition of two separate and essentially complete systems, one state and one federal, has evolved. In rhetoric and in theory, these two judicial enterprises are both sovereign—both equal and independent—except for the one point at the apex, where the U.S. Supreme Court holds appellate power over the highest court of the state. In practice, the systems are no more equal than are state governors and the president. Thus, it is that the myriad details of jurisdiction provide a deeper structure for a relationship whose theory and practice are in tension. Part of this story and its resulting balance is grounded in the way the U.S. Supreme Court's jurisdiction does not extend to state law issues. The other part contains the various ways in which federal trial court jurisdiction actually allows authority over state trial courts, although without the label of "appeal."

Adequate State Grounds

In the 1875 case of Murdock v. City of Memphis, the Court held that only questions of federal law are open to Supreme Court review; state court judgments are final on questions of state law. This question had not been decided sharply before then for philosophical reasons. In much of the nineteenth century, lawyers and judges believed that the "law" was a thing unto itself, a sort of "brooding omnipresence" that courts found ready-made by an unseen hand. The conception that state law was one thing and federal law another seemed more an embarrassment than a crucial fact of federalism.

Murdock directly asked and answered the question, generally limiting the U.S. Supreme Court's review of state court decisions to federal questions. One of the critical rationales underlying the Court's decision was that of federalism: "It cannot ... be maintained that it is in any case necessary for the security of the rights claimed under the Constitution, laws, or treaties of the United States that the Supreme Court should examine and decide other questions not of a federal character."

The scope of *Murdock*'s holding, although seemingly narrow, was complicated by some uncertainty about the definition of state and federal law. In Indiana *ex rel.* Anderson v. Brand (1938), the Indiana Supreme Court held that teachers could be fired despite tenure, concluding that tenure was a matter of legislative grace rather than a contract. If, on the other hand, the tenure was actually a contract, the state was forbidden to impair its obligation by the "contract clause" in Article I, section 10, of the U.S. Constitution. The contractual status of tenure, then, is a matter of state law but also the predicate to a matter of federal law. The U.S. Supreme Court took jurisdiction, saying in a strange almost Zen-like way that the future of state contract law was for state courts but its past was a federal matter. The practical effect of this holding was to prevent state supreme courts from creating new law merely to avoid addressing a federal question that would be subject to the Supreme Court's review. This solution may have been more illusory than practical; it was not uncommon for state supreme courts, on remand, to find ways to erode the decisions of the Supreme Court.[42]

An additional problem with the scope of *Murdock*'s holding was presented in the 1942 case of Standard Oil Company of California v. Johnson. Like many cases, the *Johnson* case presented an issue of the intersection of state and federal law. In *Johnson*, the question before the Court was whether a California statute that granted tax-exempt status to fuel sold to an entity of the U.S. government encompassed a post exchange. The Court held that, because the California Supreme Court looked to the relevant federal laws that governed the relationship between the federal government and the post exchange in its determination, the California decision had been one based on federal law and therefore was subject to the Court's review. Hence, although the *Johnson* case was brought solely on a state statute, the Court determined that it had jurisdiction to review the case based on a premise in the California Supreme Court's reasoning that lead to the state court's determination.

The principles of *Murdock* today are embodied in the adequate and independent state grounds doctrine. This doctrine asks two questions about the underlying state court decision: (1) it asks whether the state decision rests on a proposition of state law that is adequate to support the judgment; and (2) it asks whether the state decision is independent of federal law. If both of these conditions are met, the Court will deny jurisdiction to review the state's decision.

Of these two conditions, case law on the second—independence from federal law—is more settled than case law on the first. The seminal case for the independence doctrine is Michigan v. Long (1983). In *Long*, a police officer, having stopped a car for a brief investigation pursuant to Terry v. Ohio,[43] extended his search from the driver of the car to the car's passenger compartment. In the compartment, the officer found marijuana. The Michigan Supreme Court held the search invalid, relying on both the Michigan constitution and federal law, but it did not clearly state that its decision was based exclusively on either state or federal law. In determining whether jurisdiction to review the state decision was proper, the Court held:

> when, as in this case, a state court decision fairly appears to rest primarily on federal law, or to be interwoven with the federal law, and when the adequacy and independence of any possible state law ground is not clear from the face of the opinion, we will accept as the most reasonable explanation that the state court decided the case the way it did because it believed that federal law required it to do so.[44]

The Court justified its holding by referencing its respect for state courts and its desire to avoid advisory opinions, although there is also a practical justification. The rule of *Long* streamlines the judicial process, because the Court no longer has to address unclear state court decisions by vacating and remanding for clarification, a process that can be undermined by an uncooperative state court. Now, if the state court wishes to avoid federal review, it must draft its reasoning appropriately in the first place.

In assessing the adequacy of state law requirement, the Court has repeatedly focused on state court decisions, such as *Brand* [Indiana *ex. rel.* Anderson v. Brand], that seem to present a manipulation of state law to defeat federal rights. This was the principal concern of Chief Justice Rehnquist in his concurring opinion to the Bush v. Gore (2000) decision. In that opinion, the Chief Justice, joined by Justices Scalia and Thomas, noted that Article II, section 1, clause 2, of the U.S. Constitution, as interpreted by prior case law of the Court, does not permit judicial interpretation of statutes that appoint electors for a presidential election. Furthermore, the Chief Justice noted that 3 U.S.C., section 5, established a cutoff date for the Florida legislature to make its final determination of the Florida electors. Hence, when the Florida Supreme Court, in its attempt to resolve the dispute for presidential votes that was before it, ordered a recount of votes that would likely have taken the final determination of Florida's electors past the cutoff date established by federal law, the Chief Justice concluded that this new interpretation of state election law was essentially a means of defeating the federal rights of the Florida legislature. That the Chief Justice's conclusion required an interpretation of Florida law other than that provided by the Florida Supreme Court was irrelevant in light of similar cases, such as *Brand.*

The concurring opinion to Bush v. Gore refers to other clearer examples of state court manipulation of state law for purposes of undermining federal rights. For example, in NAACP v. Alabama *ex rel.* Patterson (1958), the Alabama Supreme Court affirmed a lower court's decision to hold the NAACP in contempt for not revealing the names of all of its members and agents to the Alabama attorney general. The NAACP challenged the constitutionality of the contempt order to the Alabama Supreme Court, seeking certiorari review from that court. The Alabama Supreme Court, however, refused to consider the matter because the NAACP did not seek mandamus review, which the Alabama Supreme Court then decided *for the first time* was the only available means for appealing such an order. The U.S. Supreme Court reversed, stating that its "jurisdiction is not defeated if the nonfederal ground relied upon by the state court is without any fair or substantial support." Not coincidentally, many similar cases finding state procedures inadequate arose from the Civil Rights Era.[45]

In sum, state rules are adequate when a judgment based on them "would necessarily be affirmed even if any decision on federal law were reversed,"[46] and as long as they do not violate the Constitution and are not used to frustrate a federal claim. The creation of a novel state remedy in achieving the latter is particularly questionable. A state decision is independent if it is based entirely on state law and is not tied to federal law. Rather surprisingly, these well-established practices have been followed for more than a century without any clear indication of whether they represent a constitutional obligation or simply an interpretation of the relevant sections of the Judicial Code. Regardless of whether a state decision claims to be adequate and independent, however, the Supreme Court must necessarily venture into the decision and its supporting laws—whether state or federal—to determine for itself whether the decision is genuinely adequate and independent.

THE PARITY OF STATE COURTS

Appeal to the Supreme Court from state proceedings generally must be from final decisions of a state's highest court.[47] However, when federal constitutional claims are involved, the finality of state proceedings and direct review is not always the end of the matter. Rather, the method of direct appeal is a general statement that is subject to the notable exception of habeas corpus—collateral relief sought in a federal district court that allows that federal court to reconsider the merits of any of the petitioner's federal constitutional claims heard and decided in state court. In addition, 42 U.S.C., section 1983, provides a civil means for review of state policies or actions of questionable constitutional character.

Habeas Corpus

The writ of habeas corpus protects individuals from arbitrary and wrongful imprisonment. Its origins are in English law, and, recognizing its importance in the protection of civil liberties, it was embodied in the Constitution by the Framers. The Constitution provides: "The Privilege of the Writ of Habeas Corpus shall not be suspended, unless when in Cases of Rebellion or Invasion the public Safety may require it."[48] Although use of the writ provides an alternative means of attacking state decisions and proceedings other than direct appeal, it is well settled that the normal rules of res judicata and full faith and credit do not apply to habeas corpus proceedings. This ensures recognition of "adequate protection of constitutional rights."[49] However, despite this concern, habeas petitions are not guaranteed. To have habeas review in the federal forum, a petitioner must meet three prerequisites: (1) be in state custody, (2) have exhausted available state remedies, and (3) have not made successive petitions for habeas relief. If these prerequisites are met, the habeas hearing is likely to fall into one of two categories: either the petitioner claims the convicting court incorrectly decided a federal constitutional issue that must now be relitigated, or the petitioner claims the convicting court did not decide a federal constitutional claim that should now be heard. As such, if a proceeding has the substance of some kind of appeal, if not the form, it follows that there must be significant restrictions on its availability. Those procedural restrictions define the reality of federalism in criminal cases.

To meet the prerequisite of being "in custody," a petitioner need not actually be incarcerated at the time of the habeas petition. In the 1960s, the Court decided a number of cases that indicated an expansive definition of being "in custody" for purposes of a habeas petition. In Jones v. Cunningham (1963), the Court held that a parolee may file for habeas review. In so holding, the Court noted that being on parole imposes restraints "not shared by the public generally." Similarly, in Hensley v. Municipal Court (1973),[50] the Court held that individuals could seek habeas corpus even when they have been released from incarceration either on bail or on their own recognizance. The Court emphasized the imminence of incarceration and, again, the restricted movements imposed by the state on the petitioner. In Peyton v. Rowe (1968), the Court held that individuals could obtain habeas review if any of the consecutive sentences scheduled to be served were imposed as a result of a constitutional deprivation, indicating that the validity of a habeas petition does not depend on whether the petition's success would result in an immediate release of the petitioner from state custody. Finally, in Carafas v. LaVallee (1968),[51] the Court held that a habeas challenge to a criminal conviction was not moot even though the sentence had been completed because of the lasting disabilities attendant to a conviction record.[52] Thus, if there is a state-imposed restraint on the reasonable liberty expectations of a habeas petitioner, the petitioner likely meets the "in custody" requirement.

The requirement that petitioners in state custody exhaust all available state court procedures before seeking federal court review was originally created by the Supreme Court in *Ex parte* Royall (1886). The Court's conclusion that federal courts should not entertain a claim in a habeas corpus petition until after the state courts have had an opportunity to hear the matter was based on comity and deference for state proceedings. The exhaustion requirement was subsequently adopted by Congress in the 1948 revisions of the habeas corpus statutes.

Exhaustion raises a number of concerns. For example, a habeas petitioner must pursue all available state court remedies. If a state option was once available but is not available at the time of the petition, that option is exhausted. If the petitioner seeks to raise issues in the federal court not raised in the state proceedings, the petitioner must first use any available state court collateral review procedures. Although some exceptions have been permitted when the required state proceedings would be futile to pursue, for example, they would lead to inordinate time delays or the state's highest court had recently rendered an adverse ruling in an identical case, such exceptions are not common.

As for other concerns raised by the exhaustion requirement, the petitioner must have presented any issues being raised before the federal court in the state proceedings, although new supplemental evidence is permissible. That said, the determination of whether a given argument is either a restatement of a claim previously presented in state courts or so new as to require exhaustion is often a matter of subtlety. Furthermore, the habeas petition must contain only exhausted claims. In Rose v. Lundy (1982), the Court held that habeas petitions that contain both exhausted and unexhausted claims must be dismissed in their entirety. Finally, in Preiser v. Rodriguez (1973), the Court held that habeas corpus was the exclusive remedy for state prisoners seeking release from custody. Civil actions under the Civil Rights Act (42 U.S.C. § 1983) are not allowed as a way to avoid the exhaustion requirement.

The final requirement that all habeas petitioners must meet is the prohibition against successive habeas corpus petitions. Allowing repetitive applications would utterly eliminate finality of criminal proceedings. Two seminal cases in this area are Sanders v. United States (1963) and McCleskey v. Zant (1991). In *Sanders*, the Court stated that habeas relief could be denied on the ground of repetitive application if: "(1) the same ground presented in the subsequent application was determined adversely to the applicant on the prior application, (2) the prior determination was on the merits, and (3) the ends of justice would not be served by reaching the merits of the subsequent application." In addition, the Court held that a petition alleging new grounds for relief could be denied based on a prior petition if an "abuse" of the writ had occurred. This was clarified in *Zant*, in which the Court held that an individual who had previously filed a habeas petition challenging a conviction may file a subsequent petition presenting a new issue only if the individual can show cause and prejudice from the earlier omission of the issue. In *Zant*, the petitioner, a criminal defendant sentenced to death, learned after the filing of his first habeas petition that there had been an informant in his cell. The defendant subsequently filed his second habeas petition on this new knowledge, claiming that the government had violated Massiah v. United States.[53] However, the petitioner was unable to meet the Court's burden and demonstrate cause and prejudice in the absence of the *Massiah* claim from the original habeas petition, and the Court concluded that the petitioner knew enough at the time of the original habeas petition to have included the *Massiah* claim. However, prohibition against successive petitions is not absolute: in Slack v. McDaniel (2000), the Court held that a subsequent habeas petition was not barred as a second or successive petition when the prior petition had been dismissed for failure to exhaust.

Once these rather complex prerequisites for habeas corpus review are satisfied, one common path petitioners take is to claim that the convicting court incorrectly decided a federal constitutional issue that must now be relitigated. In Brown v. Allen (1953), the Court held that habeas corpus review allowed federal courts to reconsider the merits of federal constitutional claims already heard and decided in state court.

While *Brown* still stands as the general rule, however, a large exception exists. In Stone v. Powell (1976), the Court held that state prisoners may not use habeas corpus as a means of relitigating exclusionary rule claims if the state has provided an opportunity for full and fair litigation of those claims. Central to the Court's reasoning was a balancing test between the utility of the exclusionary rule to habeas corpus proceedings (as a means of deterring police violations of the Fourth Amendment) and the likely social costs (as the exclusionary rule may allow otherwise culpable defendants to go free). Weighing these factors, the justices in the majority said they "support the implementation of the exclusionary rule at trial and its enforcement on direct appeal of state-court convictions. But the additional contribution, if any, of the consideration of search-and-seizure claims of state prisoners on collateral review is small in relation to the costs." Also significant to the Court's holding was its expressed trust in state courts as fair and competent forums for the adjudication of federal constitutional rights. Hence, whereas *Brown* states that all federal constitutional claims litigated in state court can be relitigated on federal habeas corpus, *Stone* reserves from relitigation those federal constitutional claims that have minimal social benefits and high social costs.

In addition to the exceptions from relitigation that *Stone* may encompass, the Court generally does not allow habeas petitioners to seek recognition of new rules of constitutional law via habeas petitions. Historically, many habeas petitions have been filed in light of the Supreme Court's recognition of new constitutional rights after a petitioner's conviction, prompting state prisoners to file for review of how those new rights apply to their cases. Through time, however, the Court has developed the requirement that presiding federal habeas courts must determine, as a threshold matter, whether such "new" claims on the merits can be properly applied retroactively. Hence, if the presiding federal court decides that a new constitutional law cannot be retroactively applied, that court will not need to revisit the merits of the case.

The Court's current retroactivity rule was first announced in the plurality opinion of Justice O'Connor in Teague v. Lane (1989). A "new" constitutional rule exists, Justice O'Connor said, when "[i]n general ... a case ... breaks new ground or imposes a new obligation on the States or the Federal Government. To put it differently ... the result was not *dictated* by precedent existing at the time the defendant's conviction became final." Generally, the Court has broadly defined what is a new rule and narrowly limited the scope of habeas relief. However, in Stringer v. Black (1992), the Court surprisingly found that a new rule was not being sought. *Stringer* was a capital case in which the defendant's jury instructions asked the jury to weigh appropriate aggravating and mitigating factors, and described an appropriate aggravating factor as whether the crime was "heinous, atrocious, or cruel." In a different case subsequent to the defendant's conviction and capital sentence, the Supreme Court declared such a definition of aggravating factors in jury instructions to be impermissibly vague. The Court did not at that time consider states that required a balancing of aggravating and mitigating factors.[54] The *Stringer* defendant filed for habeas review based on this intervening Supreme Court decision. The Court, noting that a "clear principle emerges not from any single case ... but from our long line of authority," the culmination of which was the Court's recent decisions, found that distinctions between the jury instructions it had declared invalid and the jury instructions applied in the *Stringer* defendant's state proceeding were immaterial and did not create a new rule. Therefore, *Teague* was found inapplicable. *Stringer* indicates that there need not be a case directly on point for a court to conclude that there is or is not a new rule; the application of existing precedent to different circumstances that are foreseeable extensions of existing law does not create a new rule. However, *Stringer* is a clear exception to the Court's generally broad view of a "new rule." As such, it may illustrate more concern with capital punishment than with the niceties of federalism.

In addition to *Stringer* exemptions, Justice O'Connor's opinion in *Teague* recognized two possible exceptions to the general rule against applying new rules retroactively. First, new rules would be available on collateral review when they "place certain kinds of primary, private individual conduct beyond the power of the criminal law-making authority to proscribe." Second, an exception was recognized for "those procedures that are implicit in the concept of ordered liberty," which is a very limited standard highly unlikely to be violated by a contemporary American state court. In effect, *Teague* substantially limits what can be raised through habeas corpus to those rights that were recognized and established at the time of the petitioner's conviction.

Habeas petitioners who are not able to meet these daunting restrictions for relitigating a federal constitutional claim will claim that the convicting court did not decide an existing federal constitutional claim that should now be heard. These requests raise issues of procedural foreclosure, which has developed historically in a similar pattern to the Brown v. Allen and Stone v. Powell decisions. However, the initial case in this matter is Fay v. Noia (1963), a classic of the Warren Court, which, although subsequently overturned, retains significance. The subsequent modern standard was announced in Wainwright v. Sykes (1977).

In *Fay*, the Court held that, unless it can be shown that the habeas petitioner deliberately bypassed the state procedures, an individual convicted in state court may raise on habeas review issues that were not presented to the state. According to the facts, Noia and two other defendants had been convicted of felony murder, with the only evidence used against them being their own signed confessions. The other two defendants appealed their convictions to the state, but the convictions were affirmed. Having exhausted their state procedures, these two defendants petitioned for and received habeas review, which reversed their convictions on the ground that their confessions had been coerced. Noia, however, did not appeal his conviction. According to the Court, Noia chose not to appeal because of the financial burden it would impose on his family and because his trial judge—who was not bound to accept the jury's recommendation of a life sentence for Noia, and had the option of sentencing him to death—told him during sentencing that he disagreed with the jury's recommendation but would abide by it because of the powerful statement of Noia's attorney. The judge also warned that he would reconsider if he had the opportunity. Noia interpreted this statement as a threat to accept the life imprisonment or almost certainly face the death penalty if a retrial was ordered and he were reconvicted. In reaching its holding, the Supreme Court said:

> Under no reasonable view can the State's version of Noia's reason for not appealing support an inference of deliberate by-passing of the state court system. For Noia to have appealed . . . would have been to run a substantial risk of electrocution. His was the grisly choice whether to sit content with life imprisonment or to travel the uncertain avenue of appeal which, if successful, might well have led to a retrial and death sentence. He declined to play Russian roulette in this fashion. This was a choice by Noia not to appeal, but under the circumstances it cannot realistically be deemed a merely tactical or strategic litigation step, or in any way a deliberate circumvention of state procedures.[55]

In the 1977 *Sykes* decision, however, the Court made it clear that the "deliberate bypass" standard of *Fay* was no longer controlling. Instead, a habeas petitioner seeking to raise issues not exhausted in state court must show "cause and prejudice attendant to a state procedural waiver." The state procedural waiver at issue in *Sykes* was a failure to make a contemporaneous objection to allegedly inadmissible evidence during trial. The Court held that the failure to raise the state-required contemporaneous objection foreclosed habeas review for several reasons. First, the Court stressed the importance of the contemporaneous objection to the fact-finding mission of trial courts. Second, the Court noted the significance of the contemporaneous objection rule to finality in criminal litigation. Third, the Court stated that the rule of *Fay* may lead to "sandbagging" on the part of defense lawyers—that is, they may hold off on their federal constitutional claims and objections in the hope of a not-guilty verdict, and if that gamble fails, raise all of their claims in a separate habeas proceeding. Such a course of action would undermine the seriousness of federal constitutional claims actually raised in state courts. This, in turn, would lead to greater error on the part of state judges and undermine the "event" of a criminal trial itself, thus impugning the dignity of the state judicial system.

While the Court in *Sykes* declared a cause and prejudice test, it refrained from defining either term. In Murray v. Carrier (1986), however, the Court did give at least a partial definition to "cause." In *Murray,* the criminal defendant's lawyer erroneously omitted issues on his petition for appeal, thereby waiving the appeal of those issues. The defendant then filed a habeas petition raising the omitted claims. The Court held that the attorney's oversight or inadvertence did not constitute "cause" and therefore the petition was procedurally foreclosed. According to the Court,

> [T]he existence of cause ... must ordinarily turn on whether the prisoner can show that some objective factor external to the defense impeded counsel's efforts to comply with the State's procedural rule.... [For example,] a showing that the factual or legal basis for a claim was not reasonably available to counsel, or that some interference by officials made compliance impracticable, would constitute cause.[56]

The Court's definition, however, was not absolute:

> [I]n appropriate cases, the principles of comity and finality that inform the concepts of cause and prejudice must yield to the imperative of correcting a fundamentally unjust incarceration.... Accordingly ... where a constitutional violation has probably resulted in the conviction of one who is actually innocent, a federal habeas court may grant the writ even in the absence of a showing of cause.[57]

Although "prejudice" has not been as explored by the Court as "cause," it seems to be similar, if not identical, to a harmless error test. Thus, in Strickler v. Greene (1999), the Court held that the habeas petitioner failed to show prejudice because he could not demonstrate that "there [was] a reasonable probability that the result of the trial would have been different if the suppressed documents had been disclosed to the defense."

As a final note on the place of habeas corpus in the judicial structure of federalism, the Court in *Fay* noted that, in some cases, the adequate and independent state grounds doctrine may preclude Supreme Court review on direct appeal, but nonetheless habeas review may be allowed. This much of *Fay* seems still to be valid and serves to illustrate that the underlying justification for the system is that constitutionally protected human liberty can outweigh the autonomy and independence of state courts.[58]

Federal Civil Rights Suit

Not all federal review of state action requires exhaustion of state administrative remedies. Title 42 of the U.S.C., section 1983, creates a cause of action against those who, acting "under color of state law" (i.e., local governments and state and local officials), abridge rights created by the Constitution and the laws of the United States. However, while section 1983 suits in federal court generally fall within federal question jurisdiction, section 1983 does not give federal courts the jurisdiction to review the judgments and decisions of state courts.[59] Hence, unlike habeas corpus, section 1983 cannot be a basis for a federal district court to *review* state court proceedings.[60] Nonetheless, the preemptive force of a binding federal trial decision in a matter of state liability that would otherwise be decided by state courts has the institutional force of an appeal. The result is to deny the power to state courts to adjudicate with finality the authority of state law. The practical significance of the proceedings is that appellate review by the U.S. Supreme Court would be rare and therefore largely immaterial to an individual litigant, whereas a civil rights action is as near and as convenient as the local federal court building. Relevant to a discussion of section 1983 are what is meant by "under color of state law," who may be sued under section 1983, what constitutional rights section 1983 protects, and what preclusive concerns arise against section 1983 suits as a result of state proceedings.

The Court first directly considered the scope of "under color of state law" in Monroe v. Pape (1961), another classic of the Warren Court. In *Monroe*, the plaintiff alleged that a group of Chicago police officers acted under color of state law when they broke into the plaintiff's home, made his family stand naked in the living room while the officers ransacked the house, and then detained the plaintiff for ten hours without cause. The Court concluded that actions taken by an officer in his or her official capacity have occurred "under color of state law," even if the officer's conduct violates state law or is otherwise not condoned by the state or an authority of the officer. As the Court observed, "Misuse of power, possessed by virtue of state law and made possible only because the wrongdoer is clothed with the authority of state law, is action taken 'under color of' state law." In effect, "under color of state law" in section 1983 is equivalent to the state action doctrine of the Fourteenth Amendment.[61]

Section 1983 allows suits against officials and governments, but there are a number of barriers to openly suing either. State governments are protected by the Eleventh Amendment, and local governments generally are not liable unless their *official* policy is unconstitutional. As a result, section 1983 suits against individual officers have become the key to implementing the underlying constitutional guarantees.

For suits against officials, the largest hurdle to overcome is official immunity. The policy for the existence of official immunity revolves around

> the injustice, particularly in the absence of bad faith, of subjecting to liability an officer who is required, by the legal obligations of his position, to exercise discretion . . . [and] the danger that the threat of such liability would deter his willingness to execute his office with the decisiveness and the judgment required by the public good.[62]

Official immunity can be either absolute or qualified. Absolute immunity is determined by the officer's function performed and not by the officer's job title. Also, absolute immunity may vary in its scope of protection, but it consistently bars all litigation within its relevant scope. Judges are afforded absolute immunity from monetary damages in rendering judicial decisions, legislators get absolute immunity from litigation for prospective relief or monetary damages over legislative acts, and prosecutors have absolute immunity from monetary damages for acts associated with the judicial phase of the criminal process.

Beyond absolute immunity lies the more problematic realm of qualified, or "good faith," immunity. Generally speaking, the level of qualified immunity afforded to a state officer is directly proportional to that officer's responsibilities. In practice, this has usually resulted in a state officer being allowed to assert that his or her allegedly wrongful conduct was performed in an objective "good faith" attempt to conduct his or her official responsibilities within the boundaries of legitimate discretion. "Government officials performing discretionary functions generally are shielded from liability for civil damages insofar as their conduct does not violate clearly established statutory or constitutional rights of which a reasonable person would have known."[63] However, in Anderson v. Creighton (1987), the Court reversed the denial of a claim of qualified immunity made by an officer who had conducted a warrantless search of a home without probable cause or exigent circumstances. In doing so, the Court stated that qualified immunity was not lost unless a reasonable officer would have known that the *specific* conduct performed was impermissible.[64] Subsequently, the Court clarified this position somewhat by suggesting that a reasonable officer would have "fair warning" that particularized conduct was impermissible as long as there was clearly established law to that effect, even if there is not a prior decision exactly on point.[65]

In addition to state officers, the Court has held that local municipal governments are included as "persons" within section 1983.[66] However, section 1983 suits against local governments can only be against an official policy or custom of those governments. Even this limited application of section 1983 does not extend to the level of the state itself because of the Eleventh Amendment. In Quern v. Jordan (1979), the Court held that section 1983 did not override the states' Eleventh Amendment immunity from suit in federal court. In Will v. Michigan Department of State Police (1989), the Court extended this doctrine to include suits against states in state courts.

Section 1983 protects people from constitutional violations. It does not displace the general tort law of the states. A claimed interest that "is neither 'liberty' or 'property' guaranteed against state deprivation without due process of law"[67] will not be supported in a section 1983 action. For example, one's interest in his or her reputation is not supported by section 1983, nor is defamation.[68] In addition, there is no government duty to act affirmatively to prevent private harms.[69] However, because the concepts of "liberty" and "property" often require reference to state law in their definitions for particular facts, it is not uncommon for alleged constitutional violations also to be state law torts. If one has been tortiously deprived of his or her liberty or property, allegedly in violation of due process, the federal courts constitutional business with the matter will be limited to whether the state has provided a meaningful postdeprivation remedy.[70]

As a final note about section 1983, although the Court had once identified section 1983 as a primary vehicle for the protection of federal rights,[71] the Court subsequently backed away from that position and held that federal law requires federal courts to give preclusive effect in section 1983 actions to prior state judgments between the parties. In Allen v. McCurry (1980), the Court held that state court litigation has collateral estoppel effect on subsequent section 1983 litigation in federal court if another court of the same state would be bound by the prior judgment. In Kremer v. Chemical Construction Corporation (1982), the Court also noted that parties may not raise section 1983 issues in federal court if those issues could have been litigated in a prior state court proceeding.

Habeas corpus and section 1983 provide a federal forum for the litigation of federal constitutional rights that stem from the failure of a state to adequately protect those rights, either in its judicial proceedings or in its official policies and actions. However, habeas corpus and section 1983 are not merely the means of effectuating civil rights enforcement; they reflect, through their breadth and limitations, larger questions of federalism. One common theme is the promotion of parity between the federal judiciary and the state courts. This concept has sometimes been described as a "myth."[72] Mythic or factual, the reach of these remedies, at their height during the struggles of the Civil Rights Era and criminal procedure revolution in the 1960s, has been reduced but not eliminated by later cases. The later cases still respect the need for some way in which the federal trial courts can perform a "reviewing" function that Article III, section 2, ostensibly vests in the Supreme Court.

SOCIAL CHANGE AND DIVERSITY JURISDICTION

Article III of the Constitution provides that "[t]he Judicial Power shall extend ... to Controversies between Citizens of different States," and between citizens of states and citizens of foreign states. This is referred to as "diversity jurisdiction." Federal courts have been given subject matter jurisdiction over these controversies even though they do not involve questions of federal substantive law. Congress has authorized this jurisdiction by 28 U.S.C., section 1332.[73] But just as Congress can authorize diversity jurisdiction, Congress can also abolish it. No constitutional requirement exists for diversity jurisdiction. In the earlier discussion of Congress's power to withdraw jurisdiction from federal trial courts, we noted that Article III refers to "*all* cases" in some clauses, thus at least giving rise to an argument that Congress must somehow vest those powers in some federal court. The diversity clause, quoted above, does not, however refer to "all cases": it is content simply to speak of controversies. In fact, several Supreme Court justices, such as Chief Justices Warren and Burger, and Justices Frankfurter and Jackson, have advocated repeal of the diversity statutes.[74] In 1978, the House of Representatives passed a bill to abolish diversity jurisdiction, but the bill died in the Senate.[75] Therefore, ever since the adoption of the Judiciary Act of 1789, diversity jurisdiction remains with the federal courts. In fact, until the Judiciary Act of 1875 conferred general federal question jurisdiction, diversity was the bread and butter of the lower courts.

The Policy Debate

Diversity jurisdiction was created to protect out-of-state residents from the bias they may confront in state courts.[76] As Chief Justice Marshall stated in 1809:

> However true the fact may be, that the tribunals of the states will administer justice as impartially as those of the nation, to the parties of every description, it is not less true that the constitution itself either entertains apprehensions on this subject, or views with such indulgence the possible fears and apprehension of suitors, that it has established national tribunals for the decision of controversies between aliens and a citizen, or between citizens of different states.[77]

State hostility toward out-of-state residents was a major concern when the Constitution was established more than 200 years ago. But does that same concern still justify the existence of diversity jurisdiction today, especially in an increasingly mobile society? Most of the problems that faced out-of-state residents in early U.S. history do not exist today.[78] For example, we are no longer plagued by the issue of whether state judges of free states will be hostile toward slave owners from slave states. Slavery and other major issues of that day have long been resolved, making discrimination against out-of-state residents far less likely. Because the traditional justification for diversity jurisdiction is far less applicable today than it was when diversity jurisdiction was adopted, many arguments have been advanced for its abolition.

Against Diversity

First, as discussed, state discrimination against out-of-state residents appears far more unlikely today than it was when Congress first conferred diversity jurisdiction to the federal courts. This seems to lessen the need for it in present society. If discrimination against those from out of state lurks anywhere, it would probably be in the politicized ranks of the legislature rather than the courts, but federal courts must still apply state statutes.[79] This severely limits any protection that federal courts could provide to out-of-state residents.

Second, federal courts are overburdened with large caseloads, which is in part due to diversity jurisdiction. Diversity jurisdiction imposes huge financial costs and consumes a great deal of time of the federal judiciary. A study performed by the Federal Judicial Center in 1988 revealed that diversity jurisdiction cost the federal government $131 million (one-tenth of the federal judiciary budget in 1988) and consumed the equivalent of the workload of 193 district judges and 22 appellate court judges.[80] It is unknown what the exact costs are in recent years, but they certainly have not decreased. So to lessen the financial impact, and allow state courts to interpret their laws, many argue that diversity cases should be transferred to state courts.[81]

Third, even assuming that bias against out-of-state residents still exists, why should plaintiffs get to sue in a federal forum in their own state? For example, if person A, a resident of Missouri, gets hit by a car owned by person B, a resident of Indiana, why should A get to sue in federal court based on diversity jurisdiction, when the purpose of diversity jurisdiction is to protect B, the nonresident? The American Law Institute has proposed prohibiting diversity jurisdiction by preventing the plaintiff from filing such suits in the plaintiff's own state,[82] but this proposal has languished without enactment. Some restrictions have been made, however, as Congress has raised the required amount in controversy from $500 in 1789, to $10,000 in 1958, to $50,000 in 1988, to $75,000 as of 1996.

Fourth, some argue that the rules of diversity jurisdiction have become too complex. Federal judges devote a substantial amount of time to interpreting and applying the various rules. This problem would be completely eliminated if the cases were just left to state courts. As Professor Charles Allen Wright stated before the Senate:

> Whether a case is properly within the diversity jurisdiction of the federal courts is a wholly useless decision point that vanishes if the case is brought in state court. This is a decision of great complexity, because the rules of federal jurisdiction are

far from being bright line rules. Lawyers can easily be mistaken about those rules, and judges frequently must spend much time deciding and writing lengthy opinions about whether jurisdiction exists. In my multi-volume treatise, my collaborators and I devote 414 pages to the rules of diversity jurisdiction.[83]

For Diversity

In spite of the several arguments advanced to eliminate diversity jurisdiction, some still support its retention. First, some argue that eliminating diversity merely transfers cases from federal court to state court.[84] Although eliminating diversity jurisdiction would save federal courts time and money, it would transfer those costs to state courts.

Second, others argue that diversity jurisdiction provides a forum for a unified system of federal jurisprudence, on which attorneys and corporations have relied. If national corporations were compelled to litigate in state courts, they would need to retain numerous local attorneys familiar with state court rules. "The inconvenience and increased costs of litigation caused by the use of correspondent attorneys would be compounded by trials held in county courthouses, which are often remote from air terminals."[85]

Third, yet others argue that there is "the educational value of having two systems in interaction."[86] The Federal Rules of Civil Procedure and the Federal Rules of Evidence in particular have been engines of reform for the states, and some state innovations have likewise been taken up by the federal courts.[87] Certainly in theory and perhaps in practice, both the federal and state court systems flourish and further develop as they learn from each other.

Fourth, although actual discrimination against out-of-state residents may not be a legitimate concern today, investors, businesses, and corporations may still fear the possibility. If diversity jurisdiction were abolished, these entities may be reluctant to invest in different parts of the country, thereby curtailing national economic growth. (Conversely, maybe the existence of diversity jurisdiction feeds these fears by legitimizing them.)

Diversity Doctrine

The rules of diversity are in part statutory and in part court created. The current statute, 28 U.S.C., section 1332, provides:

> (a) The district courts shall have original jurisdiction of all civil actions where the matter in controversy exceeds the sum or value of $75,000, exclusive of interest and costs, and is between (1) citizens of different States; (2) citizens of a State and citizens or subjects of a foreign state; (3) citizens of different States and in which citizens or subjects of a foreign state are additional parties; and a foreign state . . .

as plaintiff and citizens of a State or of different States . . . (c)(1) a corporation shall be deemed to be a citizen of any State by which it has been incorporated and of the State where it has its principal place of business . . . (d) The word "States," as used in this section, includes the Territories, the District of Columbia, and the Commonwealth of Puerto Rico.

Although section 1332 and its statutory predecessors seem to be clear and easily administrable, they do not answer certain questions. For example, the statute's language does not answer whether two plaintiffs, one who is domiciled in California and the other in Kansas, can sue a defendant domiciled in California pursuant to diversity jurisdiction. Or suppose a plaintiff domiciled in California sues a defendant domiciled in Illinois in federal court. Later, the defendant from Illinois files an ancillary claim in the same lawsuit against a party domiciled in California. The diversity statute does not say whether the new party from California destroys diversity jurisdiction.

Complete Diversity

The first major Supreme Court case dealing with these issues was Strawbridge v. Curtiss (1806). In this case, citizens of Massachusetts sued a citizen of Vermont and other citizens of Massachusetts. The issue was whether the presence of Massachusetts citizens on both sides of the lawsuit eliminated diversity, even though there was a defendant from Vermont. Writing for the Court, Chief Justice Marshall held that:

[E]ach distinct interest should be represented by persons, all of whom are entitled to sue, or may be sued in the federal courts. That is, that where the interest is joint, each of the persons concerned in that interest must be competent to sue, or liable to be sued in those courts.

Stated more clearly, diversity jurisdiction does not exist unless *each* defendant is a citizen of a different state from *each* plaintiff. This rule is referred to as the "complete diversity" requirement. All the plaintiffs must be from a different state than all of the defendants.[88]

Although the rule of complete diversity appears reasonable and easy to administer, it has created several undesirable consequences. For example, although a plaintiff from New York could sue several defendants from Ohio in federal court invoking diversity jurisdiction, one of the defendants from Ohio could eliminate diversity by suing the plaintiff and one of the same defendants from Ohio in state court. If the state court renders a decision before the federal court, the federal court would be precluded from jurisdiction. Also, if a plaintiff has a cause of action against several defendants involving the same transaction, he or she could sue the out-of-state residents in federal court and limit the same-state defendants to state court. This concurrent litigation is inefficient and costly to the judicial system as a whole. There are also many issues with corporations.[89] If a plaintiff from Missouri sues a corporation, which may have multiple citizenship in Michigan, Nebraska, and Missouri, there is no diversity of citizenship.

Consider the case of Owen Equipment & Erection Co. v. Kroger (1978), in which Mrs. Kroger, a citizen of Iowa, filed suit against Omaha Public Power District (OPPD), a citizen of Nebraska, in federal court invoking diversity jurisdiction. Mrs. Kroger sued OPPD on behalf of her deceased husband, who was electrocuted when the boom of a steel crane next to which he was walking came too close to a high-tension electric power line. OPPD then sued Owen Equipment & Erection Co. (Owen) in the same proceeding, alleging that the crane was owned and operated by Owen and that Owen's negligence had been the proximate cause of Kroger's death. Mrs. Kroger then amended her complaint to include Owen as a defendant. It was believed at the time by all parties that Owen was a resident of Nebraska, just as OPPD was. When OPPD was later dismissed from the lawsuit, however, it came to light that Owen was a citizen of Iowa, making Owen and Mrs. Kroger citizens of the same state. Nevertheless, the district court upheld jurisdiction. But the Supreme Court found "complete diversity was destroyed," because it was later revealed that the plaintiff and defendant were citizens of the same state, even though this revelation came to light late in the lawsuit. Although Mrs. Kroger and her attorneys invested a considerable amount of time and resources to pursue this case in federal court, the case was dismissed. Her only remedy was to start over in state court, assuming the statute of limitations had not run out. The complete diversity rule has long been criticized as being unfair to plaintiffs in similar situations as Mrs. Kroger, who had no reason to believe that Owen, who itself originally admitted that diversity jurisdiction existed, was a citizen of her same state.

The complete diversity rule also permits parties to engage in "sandbagging," a poker term used to describe how parties can conceal that diversity jurisdiction does not exist and then reveal that it does, if it appears they will lose, right before the end of the case.[90] For example, suppose a plaintiff from the state of Iowa sues two defendants in federal court, believing them both to be citizens of Missouri. One of the defendants knows that he is really a citizen of Iowa, but he permits the lawsuit to go on in federal court, believing he may win in federal court. If, even immediately before the conclusion of trial, the defendant realizes he will probably lose the lawsuit, he can alert the judge that he is actually a citizen of Iowa, thereby requiring the court to dismiss the suit for lack of complete diversity. The plaintiff's only recourse would be to refile suit in state court. All of the time, money, and resources invested in the federal lawsuit are thereby wasted.

In determining whether diversity exists, courts must also look beyond the nominal designation of the parties in the pleadings and realign them according to their true interest in the dispute. For example, in City of Indianapolis v. Chase National Bank (1941), a New York bank sued an Indiana gas company and the city of Indianapolis (also a citizen of Indiana). The Court held that diversity jurisdiction did not exist because the New York bank and the Indiana gas company were really on the same side. Courts must look beyond the pleading and arrange the parties according to their sides in the dispute.[91]

Note also that diversity jurisdiction does not exist for domestic relations cases involving child custody, divorce, and alimony, even if there is complete diversity. As the Court stated in 1890, "[t]he whole subject of the domestic relations of the husband and wife, parent and child, belongs to the law of the States and not to the laws of the United States."[92] Similarly, diversity jurisdiction does not exist in regard to probate matters.[93] Federal courts may not administer estates or probate wills. This exclusion appears neither in the text of Article III nor in the federal jurisdictional statutes.

There is one exception to complete diversity. The Federal Interpleader Statute[94] allows a federal court to decide all claims to a single sum put within its jurisdiction as long as there is minimal diversity, that is, where there is at least one plaintiff from a different state than at least one of the defendants. In State Farm Fire & Casualty Co. v. Tashire (1967), the U.S. Supreme Court upheld the Interpleader Statute, thereby establishing the little-used but important point that the foundation of *Strawbridge*'s complete diversity requirement is purely a matter of statutory interpretation. Congress is free to eliminate the complete diversity requirement as it sees fit. All Article III requires is minimal, incomplete diversity. One suspects that complete diversity would have been eliminated a long time ago if Congress in fact thought the diversity jurisdiction were useful rather than simply familiar.

Defining Citizenship

Various rules determine the citizenship of individuals, corporations, unincorporated associations, and class actions. Some of the rules are complicated and difficult to justify. For example, a corporation is a citizen of "every" state of its incorporation, and also of the state where its principal place of business is located.[95] Thus, many corporations have two citizenships. But with unions, and other unincorporated associations, citizenship is that of each one of its members.[96] Why distinguish between corporations and unincorporated associations? Both are often similar in form and structure, so distinguishing between the two seems hard to justify.[97] Nevertheless, the courts and Congress have continued to apply different rules to different organizations and individuals. It seems, again, likely that the rules would have been rationalized a long time ago if Congress believed that diversity jurisdiction served an important contemporary function.

An individual's citizenship is based on his or her domicile. A domicile is a "place where an [individual] has his true, fixed, and permanent home and principal establishment, and to which he has the intention of returning whenever he is absent therefrom."[98] Although an individual may have many residences, he or she only has one domicile.[99] A new state citizenship may be established by physical presence in a new place and the intention to stay there. The citizenship of a child is the same as his or her parents.

As stated above, a corporation is a citizen of every state of its incorporation, and also of the one state in which its principal place of business is located,[100] and unincorporated associations have citizenship in every state where at least one member resides.[101] If the association is large, however, a class action lawsuit may be possible, which would make the association's citizenship that of the *named members* who sue or are sued on behalf of the other members. This allows flexibility to create diversity if the class members are from several different states. An unincorporated association can invoke diversity jurisdiction by bringing a class action lawsuit and naming a representative who is diverse to the opposing party.[102] If the association is a general partnership, its citizenship is that of each and every general partner. If the association is a limited partnership, its citizenship is that of each and every partner, both limited and general.[103]

Other diversity rules apply to miscellaneous entities. With a business trust, the citizenship of the trustees determines diversity, not the citizenship of the individual shareholders.[104] A legal representative of an infant, a person who is deemed incompetent, or an estate of a decedent is deemed to be a citizen of the same state as the infant, incompetent, or decedent.[105] Why a business trust is defined by its trustee and a family trust by its beneficiary is a complete mystery. A U.S. citizen domiciled abroad is not a citizen of any state and also is not an alien. An alien admitted to the United States for permanent residence is deemed to be a citizen of the state in which the alien is domiciled.[106] However, with aliens, at least one party in the suit must be a natural-born or naturalized citizen of the United States for valid jurisdiction.[107]

Collusion

A federal court does not have jurisdiction if a party "by assignment or otherwise, has been improperly or collusively made or joined to invoke jurisdiction."[108] For example, in Kramer v. Caribbean Mills, Inc. (1969), a Caribbean corporation entered into a contract with a Panamanian corporation to purchase 125 shares of stock, in return for an $85,000 down payment, and $165,000 in twelve annual installments. But the Caribbean corporation never made any installment payments. To obtain diversity jurisdiction, the Panamanian corporation assigned its entire interest in the contract to Kramer, an attorney in Texas, who paid them $1. The sole purpose of this assignment was to invoke diversity jurisdiction. By a separate agreement that same day, Kramer promised to pay back to Panama 95 percent of any recovery on the breach of contract. Kramer soon brought suit against the Caribbean corporation in federal court. The district court denied Caribbean's motion to dismiss for lack of jurisdiction, and Kramer ultimately recovered $165,000. However, the Supreme Court invalidated the recovery, holding that diversity jurisdiction was inappropriate because of the improper collusion.

But not all forms of collusion are deemed to be improper. For example, there is no collusion if an absolute assignment of a claim is made and the assignor retains no interest in the assigned claim. Also, a person is allowed to move from one state to another to create diversity jurisdiction.[109] The party's motive is irrelevant. For example, a corporation could dissolve and reincorporate itself in another state for the purpose of creating diversity.[110] Recall also that, in class action lawsuits, one can choose to name representative class members to create (or destroy) diversity jurisdiction.

The ultimate purpose of this tour through these intricate and difficult-to-rationalize rules is precisely that, that is, to observe how intricate and pointless they are. It is hard not to conclude that this complex structure exists simply because it always has. If we were starting from scratch to design a multijurisdictional forum for litigating cases of national or global concern, it would hardly resemble this one. Although there seems to be no constituency for such an undertaking, if the United States were committed to the goal of exporting the rule of law, a judicial system that reflected global reality would be a good start.

THE FEDERAL COMMON LAW

In the long-running debate about judicial activism, one recurring motif seems to be the straightforward idea that judges should apply law, not make it. At the level of great unspoken truths, this conception of judging may be the foundation of the principles of separation of powers at the heart of Article III's regulation of jurisdiction. Congress makes laws under Article I, and the federal courts decide cases arising under those laws that Congress makes. That's what it says. Under this scheme, the words "federal common law" should be an oxymoron. And yet, the simple fact is that there has always been a federal common law, and its history reveals why the scheme of Article III will never surrender to the demands of straight and simple talk.

In Diversity Cases

The story starts with the Rules of Decision Act, adopted in 1789: "The laws of the several states, except where the constitution, treaties or statutes of the United States shall otherwise require or provide, shall be regarded as rules of decision in trials at common law in the courts of the United States, in cases where they apply."[111] Although modified in some small ways, this statute remains in force today.[112]

The second chapter opens in 1842 when Justice Story handed down the decision in Swift v. Tyson. The facts behind *Swift* are not terribly exciting. Tyson had purchased land in Maine from Nathaniel Norton and Jarius Keith. In exchange for the land, Tyson executed a negotiable instrument payable to Norton. Norton endorsed the instrument, which was a bill of exchange, over to Swift, the plaintiff in the case, in satisfaction of an outstanding debt that Norton owed to Swift. Swift sought payment on the bill from Tyson, who refused to honor the bill, alleging that Norton and Keith had not given him good title to the land in Maine. The earth-shaking question presented to the court was whether the satisfaction of Norton's prior debt constituted consideration for the negotiation of the bill to Swift. If it did, Swift could collect from Tyson regardless of the latter's claims against Norton and Keith. If it did not, Swift was going to have a tougher time collecting from Tyson.

To sort out all of this legal intrigue, and no doubt in an attempt to expedite payment, Swift filed suit in federal court in New York based on his diversity of citizenship with Tyson. Tyson contended that because no federal statute applied to the facts, and because the negotiation in question occurred in New York, that New York law must be applied. He further contended that under New York case law cancellation of existing debt was not sufficient consideration.

Justice Story seemed to doubt that New York cases were as clear on the point as was alleged by Tyson, but that was not the basis of his holding. He turned to the Rules of Decision Act and, in particular, the phrase "the laws of the several states." This phrase, according to Story, applied only to the statutes and certain established local usages of the particular state, and not to its body of decisional law. As for the judicial decisions of the courts of the state, he argued that "in the ordinary course of language, it will hardly be contended that the decisions of the courts constitute laws. They are, at most, only evidence of what the laws are; and are not of themselves laws."[113]

The underlying premise of his argument, while debatable, is also understandable. On the latter count, Justice Story made the contention that that law could not be one thing in Rome and another in Athens. The law is "The Law," an absolute body of rules that are "right" and exist quite apart from the particular place, time, or culture in question and independent of any judge deliberating over the question. The judge, therefore, does not "make" law, but rather "finds" law. In this search to "find" the law, the judge may well consider the decisions of earlier (or, presumably, contemporaneous) judges as evidence of what the Law is, but the judge does not properly look to these decisions as Law, or even, law. This metaphorical "finding" was the case whether the question concerned adequacy of consideration or duties owed to trespassers on a right-of-way. The judge seeking the law to apply is not bound by precedent:

> Swift v. Tyson rests on the philosophical premise that a court . . . does not *make* the law but merely *finds* or declares the law, and so its decisions simply constitute evidence of what the law is, which another court is free to reject in favor of better evidence to be found elsewhere.[114]

As with any other common-law judge, the federal judge chooses the right rule to apply. Given these suppositions and the attendant reading of the Rules of Decision Act, and having established that no New York statute addressed the question of consideration raised by *Swift*, section 34 simply did not apply to the case. Thus, Justice Story was free to decide the case by inquiry into general commercial law.

The principles outlined in *Swift* not only held sway in the sympathies of the American judiciary but were expanded in their ramifications. A body of law developed that came to be known as federal general common law.[115] In 1893, fifty years after *Swift*, the holding in Baltimore & Ohio Railroad v. Baugh expanded general common law to include issues of an employer's liability to an employee for certain torts of fellow employees.[116] It is the rationale that is of particular interest, and the rationale employed by the court was that it was not obligated to follow Ohio law because the liability of the railroad in this instance was one of general law. In fact, the "federal courts have an independent jurisdiction in the administration of state laws, coordinate with and not subordinate to, that of the state courts, and are bound to exercise their own judgment as to the meaning and effect of those laws."[117] The prerogative claimed by Justice Story in being free to embark on an independent investigation of the applicable law now seemed to be a duty. In 1910, *Swift* was expanded still further when the Fourth Circuit Court of Appeals sitting in diversity decided that it was not bound by a decision of the West Virginia Supreme Court regarding claims to land in that state.[118] Not only that, but the plaintiff had a *constitutional right* to an independent assessment of the law of the state.[119] Congress, the engine of making law according to the Constitution, was limited to certain specified subjects—commerce, bankruptcy, patents, and so on—but the federal courts could, indeed *must*, make law on all subjects that come before them. Neither separation of powers nor federalism could stay these judicial Solons from their rounds.

These decisions culminated in the famous case of Black & White Taxicab & Transfer Co. v. Brown & Yellow Taxicab & Transfer Co. (1928). The Brown & Yellow Taxicab Company, a Kentucky company owned by people from Kentucky, sought to enter into a contract with the Louisville & Nashville Railroad, another Kentucky company. Under this contract, Brown & Yellow was to be awarded the exclusive right to pick up and discharge fares at the train depot in Bowling Green, Kentucky. A competing taxicab operation, the Black & White Taxicab Company, also a Kentucky company owned by people from Kentucky, was less than enthusiastic about this arrangement and sought to interfere with the privilege. Knowing that a contract granting a monopoly was void under the common law of Kentucky, and that Kentucky courts would therefore refuse to enforce the deal between the railroad and Brown & Yellow, it was decided that Brown & Yellow would dissolve and reincorporate in Tennessee, and sign the contract with the railroad in Tennessee, thereby creating diversity between it and the competing Black & White Taxicab Co. It then brought suit in federal court—in Kentucky, no less—to enjoin Black & White from interfering with its monopolistic arrangement with the railroad. The Supreme Court upheld the federal court's enforcement of the monopoly, stating that it had the authority under *Swift* to reach its own conclusion apart from whatever Kentucky courts might do with the same case.

By the time of *Erie*, two big problems were apparent with Justice Story's position in *Swift*. The first was that it was quite apparent that the law could be one thing in Rome and another in Athens, or one thing in New York and another in Pennsylvania. In fairness to Story, he did acknowledge this when he noted that New York had no statutory authority for determining whether or not cancellation of Norton's debt constituted consideration for the purposes of negotiating the bill to Swift. Furthermore, the New York legislature could have passed a statute if they chosen to do so. Had they done so, the statute would have been among the "laws of the several states" that Justice Story would be obligated to follow.

Second, and arguably worse, the law could be one thing for Athenians in Athens and another for Romans in Athens (or for Tennesseans in Kentucky). This would lead to the kind of overt manipulation seen in *Black & White*. By incorporating in Tennessee, Black & White Taxi succeeded in gathering to itself substantive rights in Kentucky, rights that it would not have had were it a Kentucky corporation.

Justice Holmes wrote a powerful dissent in *Black & White*. He argued that *Swift* was premised on the impression that there is one true law, the understanding of which is the only task of any court concerned. If there were such a transcendental body of law outside of any particular state but obligatory within it unless and until it was changed by statute, the courts of the United States might be right in using their independent judgment to determine what this body of law was. But there is no such body of law. Holmes' opinion uses the occasion not only to criticize Swift v. Tyson but also more generally to articulate a positivist view of law as the will of the lawmaker rather than a body of timeless wisdom interpreted by government officials.

According to Holmes:

Law is a word used with many meanings, but law in the sense in which courts speak of it today does not exist without some definite authority behind it. The common law so far as it is enforced in a State ... is not the common law generally but the law of that State existing by the authority of that State.[120]

The position advocated by Justice Holmes in *Black & White* became the majority decision written by Justice Brandeis in Erie Railroad v. Tompkins in 1938, three years after the death of Justice Holmes. The facts behind *Erie* were literally pedestrian. Tompkins, a citizen of Pennsylvania, was walking along a footpath that ran parallel to a railroad track for some distance in Hughestown, Pennsylvania. The track was used by the Erie Railroad Company of New York. The railroad acknowledged that it was customary for citizens in the area to walk along the right-of-way in that area. As Tompkins was walking along one dark night, he was struck by an object protruding from a passing train with the result that he lost a part of his arm. Tompkins brought a diversity suit in federal court in New York to recover for his injury. He argued that the railroad was obligated to compensate him for his injuries because he was on the premises lawfully and the accident was caused by the negligent operation or maintenance of the train. For its part, the railroad did not deny that the accident happened or that it was caused by some object that was protruding from the train. The railroad did contend, however, that its liability must be determined by Pennsylvania law. According to the railroad, the Pennsylvania Supreme Court had declared that people using pathways that run parallel to railroad track are to be deemed trespassers and are owed no duty other than to refrain from willful or wanton negligence, which Tompkins could not establish. Tompkins denied the existence of any such Pennsylvania law, and because there were no Pennsylvania statutes to address the question, he countered that the federal court must apply principles of general common law. The trial court did so and returned a $30,000 verdict for Tompkins, a verdict upheld by the court of appeals and from there going to the Supreme Court.

In appealing to the Supreme Court, it was not the contention of the Erie Railroad that Swift v. Tyson should be overruled. Rather, it was their position that the law in this case turned on "local usage" and therefore should be resolved by the Pennsylvania rule and not by appeal to general common law. But the Supreme Court recast the issue, asking whether "the oft-challenged doctrine of Swift v. Tyson shall now be disapproved." Justice Brandeis answered the question in the affirmative for a number of reasons.

First, Justice Brandeis said that the interpretation given to the Rules of Decision Act by the *Swift* court was simply a mistake. According to Brandeis, more recent research into the intentions behind the First Judiciary Act revealed that the distinctions made by the *Swift* court were not in keeping with what was intended by the Act. Instead, the original Act was intended to make certain that "in all matters except those in which some federal law is controlling" the courts sitting in diversity jurisdiction would apply the "law of the State, unwritten as well as written."

Second, Brandeis noted that the practical defects of the *Swift* doctrine had become apparent, and that the expected benefits had failed to materialize. On the latter score, it had been anticipated that the accumulation of general common-law decisions by prestigious federal judges would induce state judges to recognize the rightness of the emerging consensus, which would result in a uniform body of common law being recognized. But state judges proved to be a stubborn lot, not as impressed with the wisdom of federal judges as the federal judges had expected them to be. The result was a maze composed of multiple legal standards for recurring issues compounded by the "well of uncertainties" that resulted from the inability to establish a certain line of demarcation between the "province of general law and that of local law."

The result of this was a great deal of mischief on the part of litigants and courts, as evidenced by *Black & White*. Diversity of citizenship existed, in theory if not in fact, to prevent discrimination against out-of-state parties to a controversy, but Swift v. Tyson was being used to allow discrimination in the opposite direction. The rights of litigants varied depending on whether relief was sought in state or federal court, and noncitizens often enjoyed rights against citizens that fellow citizens would not have enjoyed.

Third, and perhaps most important, the *Swift* doctrine was held to be unconstitutional because it allowed federal judges to establish law in areas where the federal government possessed no delegated power to make law. According to *Erie*, if the federal government does not have the power to legislate in an area, and the Constitution does not address the issue, the federal courts do not have the power to make common law in that area. They must look to the state for the applicable law because there is no federal general common law. In the federal courts' failure to look to state law, they have arrogated to the national government power that the Constitution reserved to the states.

Whatever *Erie* may ultimately say about the virtues of legal realism or the deficiencies of a natural law–based methodology, what it says about the Rules of Decision Act is clear. When federal courts decide a case to which neither the Constitution nor federal statutes and treaties give the answer, they must look to the state for controlling law. Stated in another way, in diversity cases, federal courts must apply the law that a state court sitting in the same jurisdiction would apply to the case. They may not decide for themselves what constitutes consideration for the purposes of becoming a holder-in-due-course, whether a monopolistic contract should be enforceable, or what duty of care a railroad owes to a trespasser. Rather than decide for themselves what is the law of Rome and Athens, they must apply the law as it exists in Rome or Athens.

But precisely why is this so? As Erwin Chemerinsky observes, the "constitutional basis for the *Erie* decision has confounded scholars."[121] It seems premised in part on an argument rooted in federalism and a limited role for federal power. Yet as Chemerinsky observes, this limited view of federal power was already waning when *Erie* was handed down. Within a decade of *Erie*, the Court had greatly expanded Congress's authority. With regard to the Tenth Amendment, which had to that time been seen as reserving to the states an exclusive sphere of authority, the Supreme Court now said that it stated "but a truism."[122]

In *Erie*, Justice Brandeis says that there "is no federal general common law" and that "no clause in the Constitution" gives the federal courts the power to "declare substantive rules of common law applicable in a state." This suggests that the rationale behind *Erie* partially depends on a separation of powers argument. But lest this be taken too far, it must be noted that federal courts often do make law, and nothing in *Erie* is so radical as to suggest that they are precluded from doing so in all cases. In handing down the *Erie* decision, the Court was making law in that it was changing the way the Rules of Decision Act had been read for at least ninety years. If Congress had been unhappy with that century of consensus, it would have been a simple thing to change the statute. Yet Justice Brandeis did not defer to Congress's legislative authority to change laws that they did not like, he changed the law himself because he didn't like it.

A remarkable thing about *Erie* is the lack of interest with which it was received. From the standpoint of any first-year law student, it is one of the most important cases of the twentieth century. It combines themes of separation of powers, federalism, and legal philosophy in a way that shapes the lives of many thousands of litigants, the rights of employees, and the enforceability of common contracts. Yet when it was handed down, the newspapers did not bother to report on it. In an oddity that seems difficult to imagine today, Chief Justice Stone wrote a note to *New York Times* columnist Arthur Krock, explaining why the case mattered so much. Only then did the nation's paper of record cover the decision.[123]

In Federal Question Cases

In the years since *Erie*, the Supreme Court has come to recognize a limited place for the federal common law, creating binding decisional precedents in matters involving transactions with the federal government and suits between states.[124] This development has not proved controversial for two reasons. First, its largely interstitial nature has not conflicted with any congressional policy. Indeed, the major function of this federal common law has been simply to accommodate the primacy of congressional power over state power when the U.S. government is involved.[125] The result has been to raise few real issues of separation of powers. Second, even when the Supreme Court has created what it calls, in the formal sense, "federal common law," the actual rules of the federal common law frequently turn out to reflect a deliberate decision to incorporate the relevant state common law.[126] The result has raised few real issues of federalism.

What has, however, become increasingly controversial is the judicial use of standards of international law as a kind of federal law. Several prominent lower court opinions have taken the bold position that international law is enforceable as part of the federal common law. The most far-reaching of these cases is Filartiga v. Pena Irala (1980), in which the U.S. Court of Appeals for the Second Circuit upheld a statute known as the Alien Tort Statute, which authorized federal court relief against torture and piracy, on the ground that "the law of nations . . . has always been a part of the federal common law." *Filartiga* involved citizens of Paraguay living in the United States who found another Paraguay citizen, also then living in the United States, who they claimed tortured and killed their father in Paraguay for his political beliefs. The lower court had dismissed the action for lack of jurisdiction, but the court of appeals reversed. Jurisdiction was established anywhere the process could be served, because torture was universally condemned by the law of nations, or customary international law.[127] But absent a treaty whose terms have been explicitly accepted by the United States, does customary international law rise to the level of federal common law and therefore become binding upon federal courts? If so, it would preempt contradictory state law.

The Restatement (Third) of the Foreign Relations Law of the United States defines customary international law as law that "results from a general and consistent practice of states followed by them from a sense of legal obligation."[128] This goes beyond commitments to which nations have agreed to be bound.[129] Rights claimed in U.S. courts by virtue of customary international law are not rights that the United States has explicitly agreed to enforce. Rather than being found in binding treaties, they are located in a body of international custom or practice in a particular area, in declarations of the United Nations, or even from scholarly pronouncements.[130]

The decision in *Filartiga* seemed to stand for the proposition that the status of customary international law as federal common law was secure. But this is both troubling in terms of American sovereignty and difficult to reconcile with *Erie*. If *Erie* is read to rest on a separation of powers argument, then customary international law should face the same disability as the general federal common law. Noting the general consensus of courts and scholars that federal common law must be authorized in some fashion by a federal source, Curtis Bradley and Jack Goldsmith argue that "nothing on the face of the Constitution or any federal statute authorizes" the wholesale adoption of customary international law as federal law.[131] A federal court might determine to apply some provision of customary international law, simply as an exercise of federal common law—just as federal courts frequently fashion federal common-law rules that are deliberately chosen to be identical to state law. But this is quite different from the court being *bound* to follow international law in the first place. If, as Holmes asserts in his dissent in *Black & White*, a law owes its power not to general principles but to its being asserted as law by the sovereign, then international law should not be binding until some authorized agency of the U.S. government explicitly decides to adopt it.[132] Under this set of assumptions, to say that international law is federal common law before being used as such by a court is circular. Hence, Bradley and Goldsmith argue in a later article that in their view the customary international law "should not be a source of law for the courts in the United States unless the appropriate sovereign—the federal political branches or the appropriate state entity—makes it so."[133]

As difficult as this question is, the harder question arises from the federalism argument in light of *Erie*. If international law is federal common law, then it should preempt inconsistent state law, but this seems inconsistent with *Erie*'s command that state law is to be applied to all disputes not arising under the Constitution or statutes of the federal government. Rather than addressing this question forthrightly, courts have gone to great lengths to find instead that international law is consistent with the applicable state law on point, or to deny the existence of sufficiently customary international law as to have binding force.

The *Alvarez* case recently decided by the Supreme Court in 2004 is one such example. In 1985, an agent of the Drug Enforcement Agency (DEA) was captured in Mexico and taken to a house in Guadalajara where he was tortured over the course of two days and then murdered. The DEA came to believe that a Mexican physician, Humberto Alverez-Machain, was complicit in the torture of the agent in Mexico. Having acquired an indictment and an arrest warrant against Alvarez, U.S. drug enforcement agents arranged to have him abducted in Mexico, by another Mexican national named Sosa, and delivered to federal agents in Texas who then arrested him. He was subsequently tried and acquitted of complicity in the murder of the agent in Mexico. He then brought suit in federal court alleging that the United States was liable to him under the Federal Tort Claims Act (FTCA) for false arrest and that Sosa was liable under the Alien Tort Statute for violation of the law of nations. The case eventually found its way to the Supreme Court, which held that Alvarez was not entitled to relief for his abduction from Mexico under either the Tort Claims Act or the Alien Tort Statute.

Under the Federal Tort Claims Act, the United States voluntarily waives its sovereign immunity for liability stemming from certain torts. This waiver is subject to various exceptions, and the Court found one of them to apply here as the injuries occurred outside the territory of the United States. The Court also rejected the charge that the activities of Sosa constituted a violation of the Alien Tort Statute. Specifically, Alvarez claimed that customary provisions of international human rights law prohibited arbitrary arrests and detentions and, because his arrest and detention were not authorized by any applicable law, they were arbitrary. But Sosa and the United States countered that the statute did no more than confer jurisdiction upon the federal courts. Without an act of Congress authorizing the particular cause of action, no relief could be granted within that jurisdiction.

The Court found that while the express language of the statute was jurisdictional, "the jurisdiction enabled federal courts to hear claims in a very limited category defined by the law of nations and recognized at common law." This limited category, however, was inadequate to reach the claims by Alvarez. From whence comes the authority to decide these limited claims? The Court doesn't completely answer this, but the majority does suggest that the answer lies in the prevailing notions of what the law represented at the time of the drafting of the Constitution. Owing to this broader notion of the common law, a notion that sounds strikingly similar to that to which Justice Story appealed in *Swift*, the "federal courts could entertain claims once the jurisdictional grant was on the books, because torts in violation of the law of nations would have been recognized within the common law of the time."

With the coming of *Erie*, the role of the federal courts with regard to these earlier notions of law has had to be reconsidered. The result, according to the Court, is that "the general practice has been to look for legislative guidance before exercising innovative authority over substantive law. It would be remarkable to take a more aggressive role in exercising a jurisdiction that remained largely in shadow for much of the prior two centuries."[134] This result is buttressed by Justice Souter's assertion that the Court "has recently and repeatedly said that a decision to create a private right of action is one better left to legislative judgment in the great majority of cases."[135]

But the "limited category" of cases in which the Court is authorized to allow private causes of action under the Alien Tort Statute is not limited to the narrow category listed in Blackstone.[136] While seeming to acknowledge that the category is both broader than those enumerated by Blackstone and subject to expansion, Justice Souter does not definitively set forth the criteria. He does say that federal courts should not accept a private cause of action under international law that does not at least parallel the definiteness and universality of consensus that are true of these historically recognized violations. Justice Souter observes:

> Whereas Justice Scalia sees these developments as sufficient to close the door to further independent judicial recognition of actionable international norms, other considerations persuade us that the judicial power should be exercised on the understanding that the door is still ajar subject to vigilant doorkeeping, and thus open to a narrow class of international norms today.[137]

Although it is not clear from the opinion what is required to gain passage through Justice Souter's door to relief, it is clear that Alvarez's claim fails to get past the doorkeeper. It seems certain that the domestic legal status of international norms concerning torture and perhaps detention will continue to be contentious.

CASES ARISING UNDER THE CONSTITUTION

In the logic of Marbury v. Madison (1803), the Constitution was a shield against unconstitutional action. Secretary of State James Madison was protected by the courts from an effort by Congress to subject him to writs of mandamus from the original jurisdiction of the Supreme Court. A different question would have been presented had Madison used a little executive self-help and torn up Marbury's commission rather than simply not deliver it. Then Marbury would have been forced to seek damages from Madison and the question would have been where he could find them. If the state of Maryland had not allowed a suit for tort on those facts, would a federal court have been willing to entertain Marbury's suit on the theory that he must have a remedy for this flagrant violation of his rights of property under the Fifth Amendment? The question, as the well-known metaphor has it, is whether the Constitution would have been as available to Marbury as sword as it was to Madison as shield.

In Bivens v. Six Unknown Named Agents of the Federal Bureau of Narcotics (1971), the Supreme Court allowed a plaintiff to recover monetary damages from individual federal officials as compensation for violation of his constitutional rights. Before *Bivens*, it was possible for a plaintiff to seek injunctive relief against constitutional harms.[138] Furthermore, the federal government used various procedural mechanisms to deter violations.[139] Although 42 U.S.C., section 1983, provided that a cause of action would lie against state officials who violated an individual's federal rights while acting under color of law, the statute did not reach federal officers. If plaintiffs sought monetary damages from a federal officer, they would be relegated to state tort law. Marbury had no sword.

Bivens would change that. In the morning hours of November 26, 1965, agents of the Federal Bureau of Narcotics entered under claim of federal authority the New York residence occupied by Bivens and his family. They arrested Bivens and shackled him in front of his family, searched the entire apartment, and threatened to arrest the entire family. Bivens was then removed to the federal courthouse but not charged with any crime. Had he been charged, he would have been able to use as a shield the remedy of excluding unconstitutionally obtained evidence. But because he was innocent, he had no recognized remedy. So he brought suit in federal court alleging that the entire incident was unduly embarrassing and humiliating, and that the officers employed unreasonable force and lacked a warrant.

The Court held that a federal law cause of action could be inferred from the very text of the Fourth Amendment and that damages have been the historic remedy for an invasion of personal interests in liberty. Speaking for the majority, Justice Brennan argued that an individual whose rights have been violated should not be left with only state law remedies—remedies that might be inadequate, or even hostile, to the federal constitutional interest.

The majority delineated two situations in which this private cause of action would be unavailable. The first would be circumstances in which "special factors counseling hesitation in the absence of affirmative action by Congress" are found. The Court found no such circumstances in the *Bivens* case and thus did not elaborate on precisely what would constitute such circumstances. The second situation would be circumstances in which "Congress has specified an alternative mechanism that Congress believes provides an equally effective substitute." This again was not present in *Bivens*, and again the Court did not elaborate on what would be deemed an acceptable substitute.

The arenas in which the newly created *Bivens* actions would be available were rapidly expanded. In Davis v. Passman (1979), the Court allowed recovery in a *Bivens* suit for violation of the Fifth Amendment. Shirley Davis, an administrative assistant to Congressman Otto Passman, alleged that she had been fired because Passman wanted her position filled by a male. In holding that Davis could recover monetary damages for a Fifth Amendment violation, the Court emphasized the judiciary's role in protecting constitutional rights. While Congress had enacted extensive legislation to protect federal employees against discrimination, the legislation specifically excluded suits against senators and representatives. The argument that this meant Congress intended to foreclose remedies in these circumstances was rejected.

In Carlson v. Green (1980), the Court considered allowing a *Bivens* remedy in circumstances in which an alternative federal remedy existed. In this case, a mother sought to recover damages from the director of the Federal Bureau of Prisons and other officials for the death of her son, a federal inmate. She alleged that her son's death was caused by gross inadequacies of medical care in the prison as well as by personal injuries he sustained at the hands of officials, all of which was alleged to constitute cruel and unusual punishment. A somewhat limited remedy was available through the FTCA.[140] According to Justice Brennan, however, there was no indication that Congress intended the FTCA to be an exclusive remedy.

Bush v. Lucas (1983), however, presented a case in which the Court was asked to create a *Bivens* remedy for a violation of the First Amendment. Bush was employed as an aeronautical engineer at a flight center operated by the National Aeronautics and Space Administration (NASA). After making public statements that were highly critical of the agency, he was demoted. He then sought to institute a private action against his supervisor, Lucas, for violations of his constitutional rights, arguing that the institutional remedies available to him were inadequate.[141] The Court refused to allow the action, noting that Congress had provided employees of federal agencies with extensive, largely administrative, remedial schemes for the redress of employment grievances, whether or not constitutional rights were involved. Such a carefully constructed and elaborate system as Congress had created ought not, according to the Court, be augmented by the creation of a new judicial remedy. Not only that, but doing so would upset the balance Congress sought to create. Justice Stevens acknowledged that the prospect of paying monetary damages might well deter federal supervisors from depriving the rights of their underlings, but that:

> Congress is in a far better position than a court to evaluate the impact of a new species of litigation between federal employees on the efficiency of the civil service. Not only has Congress developed considerable familiarity with balancing governmental efficiency and the rights of employees, but it also may inform itself through fact-finding procedures such as hearings that are not available to the courts.[142]

For the first time since *Bivens* the Court refused to allow a *Bivens* action on the grounds that it was foreclosed by the presence of alternative remedies.

In Schweiker v. Chilicky (1988), the Court refused to allow a *Bivens*-type suit by three individuals who alleged that their Social Security disability benefits had been terminated as a result of procedures violating the due process clause of the Fifth Amendment. Justice O'Connor found that the case could not "reasonably be distinguished from Bush v. Lucas." Congress had provided extensive administrative mechanisms for review and partial remedy of alleged constitutional violations within the program, and this precluded additional *Bivens* remedies. The remedy Congress had provided allowed for reinstatement of lost payments but not for other damages, much as the employment remedy for *Bush* had been limited to reinstatement of his employment.

In Chappell v. Wallace (1983), the plaintiff sought damages for racial discrimination alleged by superior officers in the Navy. Chief Justice Burger's opinion for the Court found that such a suit, involving as it did the very nature of military discipline, was a clear instance of what *Bivens* meant by "factors counseling hesitation." Furthermore, authority over administering the details of operating the military and regulating military life was vested in the Congress, not in the courts. *Chappell* was reinforced, to say the least, by United States v. Stanley (1987). Stanley alleged that, while serving in the Army, he had been subjected to experimentation with LSD (d-lysergic acid diethylamide), with permanent damage as a result. These experiments had been conducted without his knowledge or consent. The case easily could have been distinguished from *Chappell*. It would be reasonable to hold that drug experimentation is not part of military order and discipline, but the Court refused to allow the action for any injuries that "arise out of or are in the course of activity incident to service." This is true not because of any alternative remedy that Congress may afford, but because of the special place of the military.

Although the practical reality at the present time seems to be that the Supreme Court is unlikely to recognize new uses of the Constitution as a sword, two issues remain contentious. The first is whether the Court is exceeding its constitutional power when it creates a cause of action.[143] On one side is a separation of powers argument. This argument is pressed so far in dissent that, absent legislative action to authorize monetary damages against federal officers, potential litigants are left to state tort remedies.[144] The counterargument asserts that it is the role of the judiciary to provide remedies for the violation of rights, and the fashioning of remedies has traditionally been a judicial power.

The second issue is whether the availability of *Bivens* relief is mandated by the Constitution or is a matter of federal common law. If the former is true, it would be unconstitutional for Congress to attempt to preclude such remedies as those provided by statute. Conversely, if judicially recognized relief for unconstitutional executive acts is an interstitial process of the federal common law, then Congress could restrict or limit its availability. The Supreme Court has never explicitly answered this, but the extreme deference shown by recent opinions to congressional judgment and incomplete remedial schemes are consistent with the conclusion that the ultimate power rests with the legislature.[145]

IMPLIED STATUTORY CAUSES OF ACTION

Many federal statutes specify norms of behavior and establish criminal or administrative penalties for failure to conform to the standards, but they do not specifically authorize suits for monetary damages stemming from the failure of some individual or entity to comply with the statute. As might be expected, individuals who have suffered as a result of another's failure to comply with these laws and regulations have asked the courts to allow them to recover damages, and the courts have at times obliged.

The Court has taken three different approaches to these questions, each more restrictive than the former. In 1964, the Warren Court handed down J.I. Case Co. v. Borak, which is an apt illustration of the earliest approach. The issue in *Borak* was whether a shareholder of a corporation had a private right of action for damages stemming from the issuance of false or misleading proxy statements in violation of the Securities Exchange Act of 1934.[146] The Court allowed the suit, arguing that allowing the private right of action would supplement the government's attempts to prevent false proxy statements, which was the clear intent of Congress in passing the statutory framework. Under the *Borak* framework, federal courts may create a private right of action if such suits would further the legislative purpose behind a statute.

Things changed substantially in 1975 with the Supreme Court decision in Cort v. Ash, which set a more restrictive tone by establishing a clear set of criteria for the creation of a private right of action. Although the case raised other questions, *Cort* held that the existence of a federal statute did not automatically confer upon individuals a right to private relief in the absence of congressional evidence that such relief not be allowed. The case involved advertisements run by Bethlehem Steel in the months leading up to the 1972 presidential election. Ash, the respondent, owned 50 shares of stock in Bethlehem and filed suit for himself and, derivatively, for Bethlehem. Bethlehem stipulated that it had paid for the ads out of general corporate funds. The ads ran in several national publications and in local newspapers in some of the towns where Bethlehem had plants. The ads contained various allegations and featured a caption that read, "I say let's keep the campaign honest. Mobilize 'truth squads,'" and offered to send free information explaining how to do this to anyone who requested it. The suit alleged that this was done in violation of a federal criminal statute, 18 U.S.C., section 610, which regulates when and how corporations may make expenditures with regard to presidential elections.

Speaking for the majority, Justice Brennan noted that the statute did not explicitly create a private cause of action. Given this, the determination whether or not an implied cause of action was created by the statute involves several factors. First, is the plaintiff among the class of people that the statute was intended to protect? Or, put another way, does the statute create a federal right for this plaintiff? Second, is there any indication of the intention of Congress to create or to deny a private remedy by the creation of the statute? Third, would implying the remedy be consistent with the legislative scheme? And, finally, does the cause of action to be implied lie in an area traditionally governed by state law, and a concern of the states, so that creation of federal rights would be inappropriate?

After a lengthy survey of the facts of the case in light of these concerns, Justice Brennan concluded that no private cause of action was available in this instance, owing to the determination that allowing damages based on section 610 would intrude on an area of law generally within the province of the states without aiding the main purpose of the federal statute. Although the conclusion in this particular case is not of great importance in this example, the test offered by the case is. It was used by the court in subsequent cases to determine whether a given federal statute implies a private cause of action, and although it was more restrictive than the test under *Borak*, it seems to be at odds with the rationale offered for *Erie*.

In the determination of whether a federal statute that does not specifically create or preclude a private right of action should be allowed to justify such an action being created by the court, the *Borak* approach asked whether the creation of such a right would be consistent with the legislative intention of Congress. But this raises two important observations. First, the argument from congressional silence is dubious. If Congress intended that there be no private remedy in connection with a given piece of legislation, then they could have expressly prohibited that remedy's availability; however, if Congress *had intended a private remedy to be available*, they could have created one. Their silence on the issue, in and of itself, only shows that they were silent on the issue.

But what about the assertion that the Court, in allowing the private remedy, is furthering the legislative aim of Congress? This raises the second problem. If one grants that the legislative aim of Congress is easily discernable and that the Court is correct in its estimation of the impact of the remedy it allows, is the action of the Court appropriate? If the rationale supporting the *Erie* decision is rooted in the separation of powers, then it would seem that to be consistent the Court must direct those seeking a private remedy to wait on Congress to create one or to seek aid from the states.

While deemed more restrictive, the approach under *Cort* doesn't alleviate these problems. The second prong of the test is subject to the same concerns about attributing meaning to congressional silence. The first three of the prongs are subject to concerns of separation of powers. Does the Court have the right to create a cause of action without a congressional directive in light of *Erie*? This concern became the core of a famous dissent by Justice Powell in Cannon v. University of Chicago (1979).

Cannon involved a suit brought by an applicant to the medical school at the University of Chicago, alleging that she had been denied admission in violation of a federal statute banning discrimination.[147] The lower courts had concluded that no opportunity for a private remedy was available, but the Supreme Court reversed this holding and remanded the case. The Court analyzed the case under the *Cort* criteria and concluded that all four of the criteria pointed to allowing the case for recovery to proceed. Although *Cannon* adds little to the test of *Cort*, Justice Powell's famous dissent argues that the whole scheme of *Cort* is unconstitutional and cannot be squared with the doctrine of separation of powers.

Justice Powell notes that the jurisdiction of the lower federal courts and the creation of private remedies under federal legislation are to be established by Congress. "When Congress chooses not to provide a private civil remedy, federal courts should not assume the legislative role of creating such a remedy and thereby enlarge their jurisdiction."[148] Powell goes on to observe that of the four prongs employed by the *Cort* test, only one refers expressly to intent. The other three prongs "all invite independent judicial lawmaking." In light of the decision in *Erie*, Powell asserts that the expansive policymaking role of the courts realized under the *Cort* decision is illegitimate and the *Cort* analysis must be abandoned.

Powell's dissent foreshadowed a change in the Court's direction. The Court became somewhat more restrictive, although not altogether consistently. In Touche Ross & Co. v. Redington (1979), just one month after *Cannon*, the Court all but rejected the *Cort* analysis. Although Justice Rehnquist did not specifically repudiate *Borak* or *Cort*, he did assert that the Court was now committed to a stricter standard for the creation of private remedies based on federal legislation that did not specifically create such remedies. As for the specific standard, "the ultimate question is one of congressional intent, not one of whether this Court thinks that it can improve upon the statutory scheme that Congress enacted into law." In the years since *Touche Ross*, the Court has simply refused to recognize new implied causes of action without actually abandoning the doctrine. Its most recent foray into the field was Alexander v. Sandoval (2001), in which the Court refused to recognize private causes of action that might be implied as a result of federal regulations rather than statutes. This result is not in itself surprising.

COURTS OUTSIDE ARTICLE III

Article III is designed to create federal courts that are removed from direct political power. The reasons for such a commitment to judicial independence are both obvious and deep. These strictures are designed to bind Congress and, as we have seen, they do. That Congress has chafed at the system should be cause for satisfaction rather than alarm. The confounding problem is that Congress has, in part, slipped its bonds by establishing courts outside Article III, which sometimes are called Article I courts or legislative courts. These tribunals are not staffed by judges with lifetime appointments and are empowered to decide cases outside the grants of Article III, section 2. The practical reason for such courts is obvious. Some federal adjudicative body has to try chicken thieves in Guam and overtime parking tickets in the District of Columbia. But a too-ready acceptance of this practical regime could result in a body of judicial authority not insulated from federal politics and, as a result, could threaten the very foundation of constitutional order. Thus, defining what these courts may (and may not) do is the final limiting question about the nature of judicial power.

Fortunately, one recent Supreme Court case involving bankruptcy judges has provided a comprehensive review of a previously ill-defined situation. Perhaps the most prominent body of non–Article III judges in the American system is to be found in the U.S. Bankruptcy Court. But despite the fact that the bankruptcy court seems a mainstay of the American judicial scene, in its present form, it is of relatively recent vintage. Article I of the Constitution gives Congress the power to establish uniform laws on the subject of bankruptcies throughout the United States, but this is a discretionary power. Congress may establish uniform laws, but they are also free to leave bankruptcy to the states. Indeed, for much of the early period of this nation's history, that is exactly what Congress did. The various states adopted a myriad of debtor protection laws, laws that were frequently at variance with one another and sometimes invalidated by federal courts on various grounds.

Before 1898, Congress had made three attempts to establish a national system of debtor protection, each short-lived and in response to an immediate financial crisis. Each of the three acts employed judges of the U.S. district courts to hear bankruptcy adjudication. The first, the Bankruptcy Act of 1800, applied exclusively to traders and other intermediaries and did not allow the debtor to initiate the proceedings. Congress repealed this Act in 1803. In the wake of the financial panic of 1837, Congress again provided a national system of debtor relief with the Bankruptcy Act of 1841.[149] This time, relief was available to all debtors, not just certain classes. The 1841 Act also introduced, at least on the national level, the notion of voluntary bankruptcy. While the 1841 Act was more debtor-friendly than the Act of 1800, it was equally short-lived: Congress repealed the measure a mere two years later.[150] Congress tried again in 1867, this time introducing a scheme that fell somewhere between the two earlier attempts on the scale balancing the interests of debtors and creditors.[151] This measure remained in place for eleven years before repeal, and was repealed in part because of complaints about its complexity.[152]

It was not until 1898 that Congress passed a Bankruptcy Act that would become fairly permanent.[153] Although technically repealed and replaced in 1978, and amended on several other occasions, the 1898 Act provides the foundation for the modern bankruptcy system, both substantively and procedurally.[154] The latter is of interest here. The 1898 Act again provided a forum for hearing bankruptcy cases in the U.S. district courts, but not necessarily by the judges of the district court. Instead, the 1898 Act created the position of a bankruptcy referee to hear most cases. The referees were appointed by the district court judges and given the task of oversight with regard to the administration of bankruptcy cases and certain other judicial responsibilities assigned by the district court. The decisions of these referees could be appealed to the district court. The powers conferred by the 1898 Act were gradually expanded over time by various amendments. The courts exercised "summary jurisdiction," that is, jurisdiction over controversies involving property in the possession of the court. They also could exercise "plenary jurisdiction" with the permission of the district court, which could extend to issues such as disputes involving property in the possession of a third person. This aspect of plenary jurisdiction would involve, almost of necessity, the bankruptcy courts in state law controversies, because property rights and contract rights are traditionally the purview of state law.

Owing in part to a sharp rise in consumer bankruptcies in the 1960s and increasing congestion in the federal courts, Congress eventually overhauled the 1898 Act, resulting in its repeal and replacement with the Bankruptcy Reform Act of 1978.[155] The 1978 Act created a bankruptcy court for each U.S. district court that would be an adjunct of that court and whose geographic jurisdiction was coextensive with that of the particular district court.[156] Original jurisdiction over all bankruptcy proceedings was given to the district court and was to be exercised by the bankruptcy court. The 1978 Act provided that the bankruptcy court would be the court of record and would be presided over by bankruptcy judges who would be appointed by the president and confirmed by the Senate for fourteen-year terms.[157] Their pay was set by statute, and they could be removed for various reasons by the judicial council of the circuit.[158] Hence, the judges did not have the protections afforded to Article III judges. The 1978 Act removed the "summary" and "plenary" distinctions and gave the new administrative judges jurisdiction over all "civil proceedings arising under Title 11 or arising in or related to cases under Title 11."[159] This meant that the bankruptcy court now had a clear path to hearing claims based on state law as well as federal law.[160]

In 1982, the question of the constitutionality of the jurisdiction granted to the newly created bankruptcy judges was questioned and ultimately denied in Northern Pipeline Construction Co. v. Marathon Pipe Line Co. This case provides the vehicle for trying to understand some of the questions that arise from the use of non–Article III judges. In *Marathon*, the Supreme Court held that it was unconstitutional for Congress to grant such jurisdiction to freestanding judges who did not have Article III protections and that this was what Congress had in fact done with the 1978 Act. The Court postponed enactment of its decision to afford Congress time to fix the problem.[161] All this is clear and salutary. What is less clear is the reason for this decision.

In January of 1980, Northern Pipeline Company filed for reorganization in the U.S. Bankruptcy Court for the District of Minnesota. In March of that year, as part of the ongoing process, Northern filed suit in bankruptcy court against Marathon Pipe Line. The suit alleged breaches of contract and warranty, as well as duress, misrepresentation, and coercion, all of which are generally governed by state law. Marathon sought dismissal of the suit, alleging that the Bankruptcy Act of 1978 unconstitutionally conferred Article III judicial power on judges who were not afforded the protections of Article III. The United States intervened to defend the statute.

There was no majority opinion in *Marathon*. Justice Brennan wrote a plurality opinion that was joined by Justices Marshall, Blackmun, and Stevens. Justices Rehnquist and O'Connor wrote a concurrence joining in the judgment but not the reasoning. Justice White wrote the principal dissent.

Justice Brennan begins his opinion by rehearsing both the particulars of the system established by the Bankruptcy Act of 1978 and the significance of the Article III judicial provisions. On the subject of the latter, Brennan begins with the assertion that basic to the system established by the

Framers was the notion that the "accumulation of all powers, legislative, executive, and judiciary, in the same hands, whether of none, a few, or many, and whether hereditary, self-appointed, or elective, may justly be pronounced the very definition of tyranny." Motivated by this concern, and to maintain a system of checks and balances that would mitigate against tyranny, the Framers instituted a government composed of three distinct branches. The federal judicial power must be independent of the executive and legislative power, and the Supreme Court had recently found this to be an important feature of construction of the government's power.[162] The resulting command of Article III is "clear and definite: The judicial power of the United States must be exercised by courts having the attributes prescribed in Article III."

In particular, section 1 of Article III provides two specific guarantees that are critical to the constitutional system. First, the good behavior clause in Article III ensures that Article III judges will have life tenure, excepting only those who might be impeached by Congress, thereby preventing judges from being removed for decisions deemed impolitic by the other branches. Second, the Compensation Clause guarantees compensation that will not be reduced during the tenure of the judge, thereby preventing the attempted closure of the court by forcing judges to other methods of survival. These provisions serve to help ensure that the federal judiciary is independent of the other branches of government.

Bankruptcy judges under the 1978 Act do not have these protections, observed Brennan. They do not have life tenure but are appointed for fourteen-year terms and may be removed on various grounds by the council of the circuit in which they serve. And their compensation is not guaranteed, but rather is set by statute. "In short, there is no doubt that the bankruptcy judges created by the Act are not Article III judges."

Two arguments were presented to the Supreme Court as grounds for upholding the grant of authority to bankruptcy judges under the 1978 Act. The first argument was that the powers given to Congress in Article I include the power to establish non–Article III tribunals empowered to hear specialized claims that had particularized factors and suggested distinctive treatment, and that the Court has given general sanction to such "legislative courts."[163]

Writing for the plurality, Justice Brennan rehearses the three classes of cases that were presented in the appellant's arguments in support of Article I courts. The first involved a series of cases in which the Court had approved Congress's establishment of such courts in territorial areas where there were as yet no sovereign states. A second class of cases cited sustains the establishment by Congress of courts-martial because the military is an arena in which Congress is granted "extraordinary" control. The third group of cases, according to Brennan, establishes the general validity of legislative courts to administer public rights. About the first two arguments, there is little controversy. No one seriously challenges the practical necessity or historical warrant for Congress's use of territorial courts or courts-martial. But in his dissent, Justice White argues briefly that the geographic distinction that defines the first group admits exceptions. If the distinction is that Article I courts are not to operate within the states, why do the second and third categories recognize that they may do so? With respect to the second group, Justice White expresses an understandable inability to distinguish constitutional grants of power to Congress into classes that are "clearly extraordinary" and those that are not.

But the defining notion of the third class, the public/private rights distinction, is where the real dispute lies. In this regard, White begins with the *Canter* case.[164] In this early decision by Chief Justice Marshall, the concept of legislative courts is introduced and the controversy surrounding them, according to Justice White, is begun. But however controversial the rationale, the "proposition was simple enough: Constitutional courts exercise the judicial power described in Article III of the Constitution; legislative courts do not and cannot."[165]

But there are problems with this. Aside from its tautological character, *Canter* involved admiralty jurisdiction, a power specifically delineated as part of the "judicial power of the United States" in Article III. Furthermore, decisions from the territorial court were subject to appellate review in Article III courts as, incidentally, were decisions under the 1978 Act.

The principle was revisited in the case of Murray's Lessee v. Hoboken Land & Improvement Co. (1856). The plurality uses *Murray's Lessee* as primary evidence of their contention that the "public-rights doctrine is grounded in a historically recognized distinction between matters that could be conclusively determined by the executive and legislative branches and matters that are 'inherently . . . judicial.'" The principle is expounded in *Ex parte* Bakelite Corp. (1929) in which the Court, in upholding the propriety of the Court of Customs Appeals as then constituted by Congress as a legislative court, observes that the "appeals include nothing which inherently or necessarily requires judicial determination, but only matters the determination of which may be, and at times has been, committed exclusively to executive officers." This public-rights category had never, according to the plurality, been clearly delineated, but at the very least it must include the government as one of the parties. The understanding of these cases is that the Framers expected that Congress would be free to commit such matters completely to nonjudicial executive determination, and that as a result there could be no constitutional objection to Congress's employing the less drastic expedient of committing their determination to a legislative court or administrative agency.

This is in contrast to disputes between private parties, which under this scheme would be areas in which the "judicial power of the United States" might be exercised. The upshot is that only matters within the former category may be committed to Article I courts, but the 1978 Act vests Article I courts with disputes from both spheres.

Writing for the three dissenting justices, White admits the distinction made by *Murray's Lessee* and *Ex parte Bakelite*, but counters that in his estimation the use of the public-private rights distinction was done away with by the court in Crowell v. Benson (1932). In *Crowell*, the Court approved of an administrative scheme employed to determine maritime employee compensation claims, despite a finding that the claims involved the liability of one individual to another, traditionally a private-rights area. Subsequent cases further demonstrate the Court's unwillingness to maintain the public-private rights distinction as the principal factor in finding the use of Article I judges permissible, or at least highlight their inconsistency in so doing.[166] White concludes this line of reasoning by asserting that the "complicated and contradictory history" of the issue points to the conclusion that there is no "difference in principle between the work that Congress may assign to an Article I court and that which the Constitution assigns to Article III courts."

The dissent then contends that the bankruptcy courts as established by the 1978 Act satisfied these standards. Specifically, Justice White notes that (1) ample provision was made for appellate review by Article III courts, (2) no serious argument was made that the Act was an attempt to undermine the authority of Article III courts or to illicitly empower the other branches of government, and (3) the goals sought to be attained by Congress were as compelling as those found satisfactory by the court in other instances, including specific cases upholding the courts of the District of Columbia as Article I courts.[167] The extreme specialization of bankruptcy law legitimates the creation of legislative courts by Congress.

In an attempt to make sense of a less-than-clear opinion, legal scholars have offered four different rationales for the decision in *Marathon*. The most obvious of these rationales is the vindication of the text itself. The text of Article III is not at all ambiguous and is seemingly mandatory, making no provisions for potential exceptions. The courts that exercise the "judicial power of the United States" must conform to the requirements of Article III. Under the 1978 Act, the bankruptcy courts were exercising this power without the requisite conformity.

This seems straightforward enough. And it is not demonstrably wrong, but the application of this rationale to the bankruptcy courts under the 1978 Act is demonstrably selective. If the vindication of the text of Article III required striking down the 1978 Act, why do the local District of Columbia courts continue to operate under the same apparent shortcoming? Military courts, courts of customs appeals, and the various territorial courts also receive the Supreme Court's blessing in the plurality opinion, yet this seems to contravene a strict reading of the text.[168]

A second rationale is that the Act violated separation of powers. In this context, the idea is that the doctrine of separation of powers requires judicial independence. As we have seen, Justice Brennan devoted much of his analysis in *Marathon* to the provisions of Article III supplying institutional protections to guard against tyranny. According to this argument, the problem with Article I courts, and therefore with the bankruptcy courts under the 1978 Act, was that they were not adequately shielded from legislative and executive interference.

But as with the first rationale, if this is the reason why the Act had to be reworked, then it is certainly being applied in a selective fashion. Why are other Article I courts not susceptible to the same objection? Are the judges in other administrative courts somehow less prone to undue influence from the other branches of government? The Supreme Court has found, in fact, that military judges not only lack Article III protections but depend on their superiors for advancement.[169] Yet the Court has not ordered that either military judges be given Article III protections or that military courts cease operation. This would certainly seem to diminish the weight of this argument as it applies to bankruptcy courts.[170]

Another rationale relates the fairness of litigation to the litigants. The assertion here is that judges who are inadequately shielded from the potential pressures of the political realm may not be able to provide fair hearings and adjudication. But would the alternative have been any more fair to the litigants if this was to be the primary criterion? If the bankruptcy court had not heard the various contract claims raised in the course of the *Marathon* litigation, they would have been ripe for adjudication by a Minnesota state trial court. The judges of the Minnesota court, and for that matter of other state courts generally, are not afforded the protections of Article III. And many state judges must stand election to remain in office, a pressure that did not exist for the judges appointed to the bankruptcy court. Yet no one seriously suggests that state adjudication is inherently unconstitutional.[171]

Finally, there is some suggestion that federalism is the concern at the heart of the *Marathon* case. On this theory, the protections of Article III guard the states from encroachment and political interference by and from a power-hungry national government. The idea is that courts constituted in conformity with Article III will tend to act as an impartial and independent forum that will do so, if these courts usurp state prerogatives, not by political coercion but through the proper operation of law.[172]

There is certainly something to this argument, and it finds some support in both the plurality opinion and in Justice Rehnquist's concurrence. The very ability of Congress to enact rules enabling the federal courts to hear particular sorts of cases seems to diminish the weight of this argument. The fact that Congress has the authority to enact uniform bankruptcy legislation to which the states must acquiesce seems to diminish it further.

Whatever the rationale for the decision in *Marathon* may be, the result of the opinion is clear. Congress passed new legislation in 1984 that altered the operation of the bankruptcy courts and instituted the system that is in place today.[173]

Under the current arrangement, bankruptcy judges serve as judicial officers of the U.S. district courts and constitute the bankruptcy court for their respective districts.[174] Each of the U.S. court districts has a bankruptcy court. The bankruptcy court is a part of the district court, but the bankruptcy judges are not district court judges. Bankruptcy cases may be heard by bankruptcy judges or by district court judges. The bankruptcy judges are appointed for fourteen-year terms by the U.S. Court of Appeals for each respective circuit, with the total number of bankruptcy judgeships determined by Congress. Currently, there are 324 bankruptcy judgeships, including eight temporary judgeships, authorized for the districts. Their decisions may be reviewed by the geographically appropriate district court.

Section 1334 vests original and exclusive jurisdiction over all cases arising under the bankruptcy code in the district court.[175] Bankruptcy judges may hear these cases as adjuncts of the district court. "Case" in this context is a term of art: it refers to the entire pendency of the litigation, not merely some aspect of it. The bankruptcy aspect is a "proceeding" in bankruptcy parlance, a specific dispute that arises during bankruptcy litigation and may be, indeed often is, a suit under state law. The district court has original but not exclusive jurisdiction over three types of proceedings. The first are those "arising under" Title 11. These are proceedings involving rights or obligations created by Title 11. The second are those "arising in" a case under Title 11. This, too, is fairly straightforward, involving matters peculiar to bankruptcy and relating to the application of the bankruptcy code. The third are those "related to" a case under Title 11. These are matters that affect the Title 11 case but do not depend on Title 11 for their applicable law, such as the various contract claims that were at issue in the *Marathon* case. These were issues not of bankruptcy law but of Minnesota contract law, yet had to be resolved to administer the bankruptcy case.

In all of this, the district court judge retains ultimate control of the bankruptcy judge and may withdraw a case or proceeding from the bankruptcy judge.[176] Additionally, under certain circumstances, the federal district judge is required to abstain from hearing certain matters and, in other cases, is permitted to abstain if he or she believes that abstention would be "in the interest of justice" or "in the interest of comity with State courts or respect for State law."[177] Abstention moves the litigation from bankruptcy court to state court.

IMAGINING THE FUTURE OF ARTICLE III, SECTION 2

Article III, section 2, is an old structure. It assumes the existence of a common-law legal system, in which one person or a small group sues another, before one judge and sometimes a jury. The court will impose a remedy such as a straightforward injunction to do something or to refrain from doing something else. In supervising this process, the judge will follow clearly described legal rules, rules that can easily be modified by Congress. Constitutional issues will involve explicit language whose application will be clear to men and women in power. These courts will be localized at various places, set down in a nation only some of whose businesses have any connection with the national economy.

At various moments in our history, this aging structure faced massive changes in legal thought and social practice. The ideological pressures of the Civil War, with a society torn apart by, among other things, the *Dred Scott* decision, presented the first set of challenges to the rather genteel idea of judges who merely found the law. Without the miracle that was Abraham Lincoln, and the prudence represented in the Supreme Court's temporizing opinion in *Ex parte* McCardle (1868), we could have ended up with a federal judicial system narrowly circumscribed in jurisdiction and timid in composition. The crises of the New Deal, likewise, could have led us to become a nation of administrative agencies, governed by the ideals of efficiency and bureaucracy, if that can be said to be an ideal.

Today, we face potential problems of the same order. Our politics have become so partisan that debates about judicial appointments include in their vocabulary phrases like "the nuclear option." As population and litigation increase, the volume of judicial business may overwhelm traditional structures at the trial and appellate levels. The need for new trial courts will force a reexamination of the Article III model and place significant pressures on Congress and the courts to delegate matters to judges less exalted than even the most ordinary federal district judge. The complexity of scientific and economic disputes will lead to calls for far more specialization on appellate courts. The growth of global trade and, perhaps, the resulting internationalization of law itself will demand something more sophisticated than the same old diversity jurisdiction. If, as seems likely, the United States in a global arena will be an international marketplace, its courts will have to find a way to maintain the rule of law over that increasingly virtual world market.

It is daunting to think how the old model can adapt. The growth of non–Article III courts, the expansion of jurisdiction over international law as subject matter and noncitizens as parties, and increased cooperation in the legislative and administrative process, so far hemmed in by the law of standing, seem the likely direction. It will become increasingly necessary to understand the subject of this book as a historical metaphor rather than a practical plan for judicial administration. Still, it is a glorious metaphor.

NOTES

1. "Congressional Power to Curtail Federal Court Jurisdiction: An Opinionated Guide to the Ongoing Debate," 36 *Stan. L. Rev.* 895 (1984).

2. The Federalist No. 78, at 463, 466 (Alexander Hamilton) (New York: Signet, Clinton Rossiter ed., 1999).

3. "A Neo-Federalist View of Article III: Separating the Two Tiers of Federal Jurisdiction," 65 *Boston U.L. Rev.* 205 (1985).

4. *Ex parte* McCardle, 74 U.S. 506, 514 (1868).

5. After the Hamdan decision, Congress adopted the Military Commissions Act of 2006 (120 stat. 2600). This act does apply retroactively to strip habeas corpus jurisdiction in Guantanamo detainee cases.

6. Paul Lund, "The Decline of Federal Common Law," 76 *B.U.L. Rev.* 895, 930 (1996).

7. See, e.g., John T. Cross, "Congressional Power to Extend Federal Jurisdiction to Disputes Outside Article III: A Critical Analysis from the Perspective of Bankruptcy," 87 *Nw. L. Rev.* 1188, 1214 (1993) (discussing how theories of protective jurisdiction apply to bankruptcy).

8. Section 301 of the Labor Management Relations Act of 1947 provides, "Suits for violation of contracts between an employer and a labor organization representing employees in an industry affecting commerce ... may be brought in any district court of the United States having jurisdiction of the parties, without respect the amount in controversy, and without regard to the citizenship of the parties.... Any such labor organization may sue or be sued ... in the courts of the United States."

9. Some states did not grant relief to unions when an employer violated certain contract provisions.

10. See, e.g., Henry Hart & Herbert Wechsler, *The Federal Courts and the Federal System* 744–47 (1953).

11. Paul J. Mishkin, "The Federal 'Question' in the District Courts," 53 *Colum. L. Rev.* 157 (1953).

12. See *supra* note 11, Frankfurter dissenting (discussing Osborn and the Pacific Railroad Removal Cases).

13. Hepburn & Dundas v. Ellzey, 6 U.S. (2 Cranch) 445 (1805).

14. Recall that the Constitution provides that "[t]he judicial Power shalt extend to all Cases ... between citizens of different States." No diversity of citizenship literally existed in accordance with the Constitution because the District of Columbia is not a state within the meaning of the Constitution.

15. The Court of Claims hears suits involving disputed debt claims of the United States.

16. Glidden Co. v. Zdanok, 370 U.S. 539 (1962).

17. O'Donoghue v. United States, 289 U.S. 516 (1933).

18. Foreign Sovereignty Immunity Act of 1976, 28 U.S.C. § 1330.

19. Verlinden B.V. v. Central Bank of Nigeria, 461 U.S. 480, 497 (1983).

20. See 42 U.S.C. §§ 2210, 2014.

21. 461 U.S. 574, 577–79 (1983).

22. Allen v. Wright, 468 U.S. 737, 760 (1984) (quoting Laird v. Tatum, 408 U.S. 1, 15) (1972).

23. *Id.* at 761.

24. 16 U.S.C. § 1536.

25. Compare Vermont Agency of Natural Resources v. United States, 529 U.S. 765 (2000) (holding that Congress has the power to create "qui tam" actions, by which citizens can sue to obtain damages, or bounties, on behalf of the United States to recover damages done to the United States).

26. See Cass R. Sunstein, "What's Standing After Lujan? Of Citizen Suits, 'Injuries,' and Article III," 91 *Mich. L. Rev.* 163, 209–15 (1992).

27. *Id.* at 578.

28. See also Federal Election Commission v. Akins, 524 U.S. 11 (1998) (noting that a plaintiff's injury must be within the statutory zone of interest and not be too generalized or shared by all or almost all citizens).

29. 5 U.S.C. § 551.

30. See Shelley v. Kraemer, 334 U.S. 1 (1948).

31. See Pierce v. Society of Sisters, 268 U.S. 510 (1925); Runyon v. McCrary, 427 U.S. 160 (1976).

32. Moore v. New York Cotton Exchange, 270 U.S. 593 (1926).

33. Erwin Chemerinsky, *Federal Jurisdiction* 330 (Gaithersburg, NY: Aspen, 4th ed., 2003).

34. Hurn v. Oursler, 289 U.S. 238 (1933).

35. 383 U.S. 715 (1966).

36. United Mine Workers of America v. Gibbs, 383 U.S. 715, 726 (1966).

37. 28 U.S.C. § 1367.

38. *Id.*

39. City of Chicago v. International College of Surgeons, 118 S.Ct. 523, 533–34 (1997).

40. See, e.g., Evra Corp. v. Swiss Bank Corp., 673 F.2d 951 (7th Cir. 1982) (permitting a third-party defendant to file a claim against a nondiverse party).

41. § 1367(c) allows district courts to decline exercising supplemental jurisdiction if "(1) the claim raises a novel or complex issue of state law; (2) the claim substantially predominates over the claims or claims over which the district court has original jurisdiction; (3) the district court has dismissed all claims over which it has original jurisdiction; (4) in exceptional cases, where there are other compelling reasons for declining jurisdiction."

42. See, e.g., State *ex rel.* Anderson v. Brand, 13 N.E.2d 955 (Ind. 1938). This reality may have put the Supreme Court in the uncomfortable position of feeling that it was issuing advisory opinions, which would violate the cases and controversies requirement of Article III. See Herb v. Pitcairn, 324 U.S. 117, 125–26 (1945).

43. 392 U.S. 1 (1968).

44. Michigan v. Long, 463 U.S. 1032, 1040–41 (1983).

45. See, e.g., Henry v. Mississippi, 379 U.S. 443 (1965); NAACP v. Alabama *ex rel.* Flowers, 377 U.S. 288 (1964); Wright v. Georgia, 373 U.S. 284 (1963); Williams v. Georgia, 349 U.S. 375 (1955).

46. Richard A. Matasar & Gregory S. Bruch, "Procedural Common Law, Federal Jurisdictional Policy, and Abandonment of the Adequate and Independent State Grounds Doctrine," 86 *Colum. L. Rev.* 1291, 1292 n.2 (1986).

47. The Court's limitation in this matter is imposed by Congress, not the Constitution. See 28 U.S.C. § 1257.

48. U.S. Constitution, Art. I, § 9, cl. 2. The federal statutes enacting the power of habeas corpus are 28 U.S.C. §§ 2254, 2255. The Court has "long recognized that the power to award the writ by any of the courts of the United States must be given by the written law, and [the Court has] likewise recognized that judgments about the proper scope of the writ are normally for Congress to make." Felker v. Turpin, 518 U.S. 651, 664 (1996) (internal quotations and citations omitted). Hence, writs of habeas corpus, from an Article III perspective, are within the Court's appellate jurisdiction; as such, the Court will take a prudential approach to the writs according to congressional regulation. See U.S. Constitution, Art. III, § 2, cl. 2.

49. Kaufman v. United States, 394 U.S. 217, 226 (1969).

50. 411 U.S. 345 (1973).

51. 391 U.S. 234 (1968).

52. See also Lane v. Williams, 455 U.S. 624 (1982) (holding that an individual attacking a sentence—not a conviction—could not seek habeas relief when the sentence had been fully served and there were no collateral consequences that could be eliminated by a successful attack on the sentence).

53. 377 U.S. 201 (1964) (holding that the government may not, in the absence of counsel, deliberately elicit statements from a person under indictment).

54. See Clemons v. Mississippi, 494 U.S. 738 (1990); Maynard v. Cartwright, 486 U.S. 356 (1988).

55. Fay v. Noia, 372 U.S. 391, 439 (1963).

56. Notably, the Court has held that ineffective assistance of counsel claims are not procedurally foreclosed, although they may not be raised on direct appeal, at least for federal convictions. Massaro v. United States, 538 U.S. 500 (2003).

57. (Internal quotations and citations omitted). The Court has held that, to demonstrate actual innocence, the petitioner must "show by clear and convincing evidence that, but for the constitutional error, no reasonable juror would have found the petitioner eligible for the death penalty under ... state law." Sawyer v. Whitley, 505 U.S. 333, 336 (1992). However, in Schlup v. Delo, 513 U.S. 298, 327 (1995), the Court held that a habeas petitioner claiming actual innocence need only show that a constitutional violation "probably resulted" in a conviction.

58. See Trest v. Cain, 522 U.S. 87 (1997).

59. This is known as the Rooker-Feldman doctrine, for the two Supreme Court cases that created the rule. See Rooker v. Fidelity Trust Co., 263 U.S. 413 (1923); D.C. Court of Appeals v. Feldman, 460 U.S. 462 (1983).

60. Before 1973, there was tension between section 1983 and habeas corpus, as state prisoners that had not exhausted their state procedures could alternatively file a section 1983 action seeking an injunction against state imprisonment. However, this tension was resolved in Preiser v. Rodriguez, 411 U.S. 475 (1973), which held that habeas corpus was the exclusive means for state prisoners to seek release.

61. Lugar v. Edmondson Oil Co., 457 U.S. 922, 929 (1982). This makes sense, as Congress's authority for enacting section 1983 arises from section 5 of the Fourteenth Amendment.

62. Scheuer v. Rhodes, 416 U.S. 232, 240 (1974).

63. Harlow v. Fitzgerald, 457 U.S. 800, 818 (1982).

64. Anderson involved an FBI agent rather than a state police officer. Technically, therefore, this was not a suit under section 1983, which applies to state and local (but not federal) officials. Federal agents are subject to similar suits directly under the Constitution itself, however, and the doctrine of official immunity, which here is the issue, is comparable.

65. Hope v. Pelzer, 536 U.S. 730, 739–41 (2002).

66. See Monell v. Dep't of Soc. Servs., 436 U.S. 658 (1978).

67. Paul v. Davis, 424 U.S. 693 (1976).

68. Siegert v. Gilley, 500 U.S. 226 (1991).

69. DeShaney v. Winnebago County Dep't of Soc. Servs., 489 U.S. 189 (1989).

70. See, e.g., Hudson v. Palmer, 468 U.S. 517 (1984); Parratt v. Taylor, 451 U.S. 527 (1981).

71. See Mitchum v. Foster, 407 U.S. 225, 242 (1972).

72. Burt Neuborne, "The Myth of Parity," 90 *Harv. L. Rev.* 1105 (1977).

73. "The district courts shall have original jurisdiction of all civil actions where the matter in controversy exceeds the sum or value of $75,000, exclusive of interest and costs, and is between ... citizens of different States ... [and] citizens of different States and in which citizens or subjects of a foreign state are additional parties ... [and] a foreign state ... as plaintiff and citizens of a State or of different states."

74. See, e.g., Earl Warren, 36th Annual Meeting, 1959 *A.L.I. Proc.* 27–43; Warren E. Burger, Annual Report on the State of the Judiciary, 62 *A.B.A. J.* 443, 444 (1976); Lumbermen's Mutual Casualty Co. v. Elbert, 348 U.S. 48, 54 (1954) (Frankfurter, J., concurring); Robert Houghwout Jackson, *The Supreme Court in the American System of Government* 38 (1955) ("in my judgment, the greatest contribution that Congress could make to the orderly administration of justice in the United States would be to abolish the jurisdiction of the federal courts, which is based solely on the ground that the litigants are citizens of different states").

75. H.R. 9622, 95th Cong., 2d Sess. (1978).

76. Some commentators have offered alternative rationales for the creation of diversity jurisdiction. See, e.g., Henry J. Friendly, "The Historic Basis of Diversity Jurisdiction," 41 *Harv. L. Rev.* 483 (1928) (arguing that diversity jurisdiction was actually created to protect interstate commerce, mitigate the effect of states adopting antibusiness laws, and accommodate the fear that state judges, who did not have life tenure, would be susceptible by local sentiments and be hostile toward merchants).

77. Bank of United States v. Deveaux, 9 U.S. (5 Cranch) 61, 87 (1809).

78. See, e.g., Charles Alan Wright, *Law of Federal Courts* 146–152 (5th ed., 1994) (arguing state court discrimination is no longer a serious concern).

79. Erie Railroad v. Tompkins, 304 U.S. 64 (1938).

80. Debra Lyn Bassett, "The Hidden Bias in Diversity Jurisdiction," 81 *Wash. U. L. Q.* 119 (2003).

81. See, e.g., Thomas D. Rowe, "Abolishing Diversity Jurisdiction: Positive Side Effects and Potential for Further Reforms," 92 *Harv. L. Rev.* 963 (1979) (discussing the burden that diversity jurisdiction places on federal courts, and why these cases should be dealt with in state courts).

82. American Law Institute, *Study of the Division of Jurisdiction Between State and Federal Courts* 10–14 (Washington: ALI, 1969).

83. Hearings before the Subcommittee on Improvements in Judicial Machinery of the Committee on the Judiciary, United States Senate, 95th Cong., 2d Sess. 45–48 (1978).

84. See, e.g., John P. Frank, "The Case for Diversity Jurisdiction," 16 *Harv. J. Legis.* 403 (1979) (arguing diversity jurisdiction still offers multiple benefits).

85. See, e.g., Adrienne Marsh, "Diversity Jurisdiction: Scapegoat of Overcrowded Federal Courts," 48 *Brooklyn L. Rev.* 197 (1982) (advancing that individuals and corporations have come to rely on federal courts).

86. See Frank, *Case for Diversity.*

87. *Id.*

88. This rule does not prevent plaintiffs from the same state from suing defendants from a different state pursuant to diversity jurisdiction.

89. See *infra* notes 29–31 and accompanying text.

90. Federal courts are required to dismiss a lawsuit at any time that it is revealed that diversity jurisdiction does not exists, even if this comes to light near the end of the lawsuit.

91. City of Dawson v. Columbia Ave. Sav. Fund, 197 U.S. 178, 180 (1905).

92. *In re* Burrus, 136 U.S. 586, 593–94 (1890).

93. Marshall v. Marshall, 126 Sup. Ct. 1735 (2006).

94. 28 U.S.C. § 1335.

95. 28 U.S.C. § 1332(c).

96. See, e.g., United Steelworkers of America, AFL-CIO v. R.H. Bouligny, Inc., 382 U.S. 145 (1965) (holding that unions have citizens in each state where members reside).

97. *Id.* (reciting various arguments that the differences between corporations and unincorporated associations are "inadequate and irrelevant"). In 2005, Congress provided that unincorporated associations are citizens of their state of organization and of their principal state of business. This definiton, quite oddly, only applies in a class action. 28 U.S.C. § 1332(d)(10).

98. 13 B. Charles A. Wright et al., *Federal Practice and Procedure* § 3612 (2nd ed., 1984).

99. Steigleder v. McQuesten, 198 U.S. 141 (1905).

100. 28 U.S.C. § 1332(c). In the modern world, it is rare for one corporation to be incorporated in more than one state, but this practice was common in the nineteenth century, especially for railroads.

101. See, e.g., United Steelworkers v. R.H. Bouligny, 382 U.S. 145 (1965) (holding a labor union is a citizen of every state where one of its members is a citizen).

102. See, e.g., Kerney v. Fort Griffin Fandangle Assn., 624 F.2d 717 (5th Cir. 1980).

103. Carden v. Arkoma Associates, 494 U.S. 185 (1990).

104. Navarro Savings v. Lee, 446 U.S. 458 (1980).

105. 28 U.S.C. § 1332(c)(2).

106. 28 U.S.C. §1332(a).

107. Saadeh v. Farouki, 107 F.3d 52 (D.C. Cir. 1997).

108. 28 U.S.C. § 1359.

109. Note that diversity jurisdiction is created at the time the complaint is filed, not when the events arose that gave rise to the lawsuit.

110. See, e.g., Black & White Taxicab & Transfer Co. v. Brown & Yellow Taxicab Co., 276 U.S. 518, 524 (1928).

111. Rules of Decision Act, 1 Stat. 92 (1789).

112. 28 U.S.C. § 1652 (the phrase "trials at common law" from the 1789 Act has been changed to read "civil cases" in the current statute).

113. 41 U.S. at 18.

114. W. Casto, "The Erie Doctrine and the Structure of Constitutional Revolutions," 62 *Tul. L. Rev*. 907, 913 (1988).

115. Federal general common law is distinguished from other federal common law that is based on decisions involving federal statutory authority. The ability of the federal courts to decide issues related to the application of federal statutes is a different issue altogether. This federal general common law applied to issues in federal court that did not turn on federal questions, that is, to situations in which the federal court is sitting in diversity jurisdiction.

116. Baltimore & Ohio Railroad v. Baugh, 149 U.S. 368 (1893), holding under the fellow servant rule that the Baltimore & Ohio was not liable to Baugh, their employee, for injuries he sustained when a coworker negligently caused a collision in moving a locomotive contrary to company policy, because the Baltimore & Ohio company was not itself negligent.

117. *Id.* at 372. The court in *Baltimore & Ohio RR* continued to briefly explore the potential difficulties attendant with such a system of dual sovereigns that could

potentially apply two different rules and noted the need for a generalized deference. This is beyond the scope of the present treatment, except to say that they recognized, if not a philosophical problem, at least the very real potential for problems of exigency.

118. Kuhn v. Fairmont Coal Co., 215 U.S. 349 (1910). Justice Harlan noted that deference to the state decision would be called for if the issues had been of settled law at the time in question, but such was not the case. *Id.* at 364. Of course, being required to give *deference* to state decisions is far from being *required to follow* state decisions.

119. *Id.* at 366.

120. Black & White Taxicab Co. v. Brown & Yellow Taxicab Co., 276 U.S. 518, 533–34 (1928).

121. Erwin Chemerinsky, *Federal Jurisdiction* 315 (Gaithersburg, NY: Aspen, 4th ed., 2003).

122. *Id.*, quoting United States v. Darby, 312 U.S. 100, 124 (1941).

123. Alpheus T. Mason, *Harlan Fiske Stone: Pillar of the Law* 476–77 (New York: Viking, 1956).

124. Martha Field, "Sources of Law: The Scope of Federal Common Law," 99 *Harv. L. Rev.* 991 (1986).

125. United States v. Little Lake Misere Land Co., 412 U.S. 580 (1973).

126. United States v. Kimball Foods, Inc., 440 U.S. 715 (1979).

127. 630 U.S. 876. The "law of nations" and "customary international law" are not synonymous terms, the former encompasses the latter but historically would have included admiralty law and the law of merchant, and so on, as well.

128. Restatement 3rd Foreign Relations Law of the United States § 102(2) (1987). Although often quite influential, Restatements are not, in themselves, law and therefore are not binding in courts.

129. Even in the case of specific ratification of a treaty, treaties generally are not self-executing. Congress must define and implement the obligations through legislation, and this legislation then becomes the rule of decision that is binding on the courts.

130. Peter W. Low and John C. Jeffries, Jr., *Federal Courts and the Law of Federal-State Relations* 226–27 (New York: Foundation Press, 5th ed., 2004). The doctrine of the "persistent objector" affords the state an opportunity to avoid being bound by customary international law if it takes the proper, active steps. *Id.*

131. Curtis A. Bradley and Jack L. Goldsmith, "Customary International Law as Federal Common Law: A Critique of the Modern Position," 110 *Harv. L. Rev.* 815, 856–57 (1997). For the opposing argument, see Harold Hongju Koh, "Is International Law Really State Law?" 111 *Harv. L. Rev.* 1824 (1998).

132. 276 U.S. at 533, Justice Holmes, dissenting. To the extent that customary international law is found in pronouncements from extranational bodies such as the United Nations, the force of this argument may be affected to the extent that these bodies may be deemed to be sovereigns. But it would still seem that, according to Holmes' view, some congressional commitment would be needed to bind the government.

133. Curtis A. Bradley and Jack L. Goldsmith, "Federal Courts and the Incorporation of International Law," 111 *Harv. L. Rev.* 2260 (1998).

134. Sosa v. Alvarez-Machain, 542 U.S. 692, 726 (2004).

135. *Id.* at 727.

136. Blackstone cited three crimes recognized in England as against the "laws of nations" and subject to a body of judge-made laws affecting the obligations of

individuals outside of England: piracy, violation of safe conducts, and infringement on ambassadors. 4 William Blackstone. *Commentaries on the Laws of England* 68 (1766).

137. *Id.* at 729.

138. This stems from the decision in *Ex parte* Young, 209 U.S. 123 (1908). Interestingly, this was deemed to exist even in the absence of express statutory authority.

139. As, for example, with the exclusionary rule, which precludes the government from introducing at trial evidence obtained against a defendant in violation of that defendant's constitutional rights. See Mapp v. Ohio, 367 U.S. 643 (1961).

140. 28 U.S.C. § 2680.

141. After roughly two years of institutional review, Bush had been reinstated with backpay.

142. 462 U.S. at 389.

143. The differences in *Bivens* between the majority and the dissent largely turn on their response to this issue.

144. See Carlson v. Green, 446 U.S. 14, 51 (1980) (Rehnquist, J., dissenting).

145. See Chemerinsky, *Federal Jurisdiction*, 601–604 (Gaithersburg, NY: Aspen, 4th ed., 2003).

146. Specifically, section 14(a) of the Securities Exchange Act of 1934, 48 Stat. 895, 15 U.S.C. § 78(n)(a).

147. Specifically, section 901 of Title IX of the Education Amendments of 1972, 20 U.S.C.S. § 1681.

148. Cannon v. University of Chicago, 441 U.S. 677, 730–31 (1979).

149. 5 Stat. 440.

150. Charles Warren, *Bankruptcy in United States History* 81–85 (Cambridge: Harvard University Press, 1935).

151. 14 Stat. 517.

152. David A. Moss, *When All Else Fails: Government as the Ultimate Risk Manager* 137 (Cambridge: Harvard University Press, 2002).

153. 92 Stat. 2549.

154. 30 Stat. 544.

155. 92 Stat. 2657.

156. 28 U.S.C.S. § 151.

157. 28 U.S.C.S. §§ 151–153

158. *Id.*

159. The current bankruptcy code, that is, the substantive law of bankruptcy, is found in Title 11 of the United States Code.

160. 28 U.S.C.S. § 1481.

161. The Court stayed judgment until October 4, 1982, to give Congress time to correct the problems. Congress passed an emergency rule (this is called "kicking the can down the road") to enable the bankruptcy courts to continue to operate until new legislation was put into place in 1984.

162. 458 U.S. at 58, citing United States v. Will, 449 U.S. 200, 217–218 (1980).

163. 458 U.S. at 62, referring to Palmore v. United States, 411 U.S. 389 (1973), at 408. The second argument was that bankruptcy courts established by the act were mere adjuncts of the district court and were, therefore, legitimate. Needless to say, the plurality found this unpersuasive.

164. American Ins. Co. v. Canter, 26 U.S. (1 Pet.) 511 (1828). The case involved Congress's establishment of territorial courts in the area that is now the state of Florida.

165. Northern Pipeline Constr. Co. v. Marathon Pipe Line Co., 458 U.S. 50, 106 (1982).

166. Williams v. United States, 289 U.S. 553 (1933), considering the Court of Claims; O'Donoghue v. United States, 289 U.S. 516 (1933), considering the courts of the District of Columbia; National Mutual Insurance Co. v. Tidewater Transfer Co., Inc., 337 U.S. 582 (1949), with no majority opinion—the plurality upheld a statute giving D.C. courts the right to hear suits between citizens of the District of Columbia and those of a state.

167. Palmore v. United States, 411 U.S. 389 (1973).

168. 458 U.S. at 64–70.

169. See O'Callahan v. Parker, 395 U.S. 258, 264 (1969).

170. Martin Redish, "Legislative Courts, Administrative Agencies, and the *Northern Pipeline* Decision," 1983 *Duke L.J.* 197 (1983).

171. Low and Jeffries, *Federal Courts*, 315.

172. See Lucinda Finley, "Article III Limits on Article I Courts: The Constitutionality of the Bankruptcy Court and the 1979 Magistrate Act," 80 *Colum. L. Rev.* 560, 582–83 (1980). Cited in Low and Jefferies, *Federal Courts*, 315.

173. The much publicized 2005 amendments to the Bankruptcy Act largely affected the substantive law of bankruptcy and not the actual operation of the courts.

174. While the substantive bankruptcy law is found in Title 11 of the United States Code, the procedural rules, including issues discussed in this paragraph, are found in Title 28, and particularly in sections 151, 157, and 1334.

175. 28 U.S.C.A. § 1334(a).

176. 28 U.S.C.A. § 157(d).

177. 28 U.S.C.A. § 1334(c)2, and 28 U.S.C.A. § 1334(c)1, respectively.

Bibliographic Essay

AN INTRODUCTORY NOTE ABOUT IDEOLOGY

One book, in many editions, has defined the basic theoretical approach to this subject. Usually simply called "Hart & Wechsler," now in a fifth edition as Richard H. Fallon, Jr., Daniel J. Meltzer, and David L. Shapiro, *Hart and Wechsler's The Federal Courts and the Federal System* (New York: Foundation Press, 5th ed., 2003), this powerful work of scholarship is, in theory, a law school teaching book; however, in reality, it has become the starting point, and often the ending point as well, for scholarship and analysis about the law of federal judicial power. Philosophically, especially in its original 1953 edition, this work is a mainstay of the view of law as a neutral and principled force at the center of our institutional processes.

The magisterial force of this great work needs to be respected by the unwary. An insightful article by Judith Resnick, "Rereading 'The Federal Courts': Revising the Domain of Federal Courts Jurisprudence at the End of the Twentieth Century," 47 *Vand. L. Rev.* 1021 (1994), will help the reader gain perspective on the Hart and Wechsler vision. Similarly, a work by the distinguished federal judge and scholar Richard A. Posner, *The Federal Courts: Crisis and Reform* (Cambridge: Harvard, 1996), approaches the subject from a systematically pragmatic point of view. And Charles G. Geyh's *When Courts and Congress Collide: The Struggle for Control of America's Judicial System* (Ann Arbor: University of Michigan Press, 2006) is a useful reminder that much of the subject has been driven by the very unphilosophical forces of partisanship and political advantage. Finally, the reader who is seeking to understand the basic subject in terms of law and public policy, and to see the relationship between the parts and the whole, should turn to Erwin Chemerinsky, *Federal Jurisdiction* (New York: Aspen, 4th ed., 2003).

PART I: A HISTORY OF THE FEDERAL COURT SYSTEM

Colonial Courts and the Articles of Confederation. The definitive general history of this period from the standpoint of constitutionalism is Gordon Wood, *The Creation of the American Republic, 1776–1787* (Chapel Hill, NC: University of North Carolina Press, 1969). The most useful overview of the courts leading up the Constitution is John P. Frank, "Historical Bases of the Federal Judicial System," 13 *Law and Contemporary Problems* 3 (1948). An important history of the Supreme Court devotes considerable attention to the early history of the American court system. Julius Goebel, *History of the Supreme Court of the United States: Antecedents and Beginnings to 1801* (New York: Macmillan, 1971).

The Constitutional Convention and Ratification. There is no complete book-length study of the judicial article at the Convention. The standard account can be found in Charles Warren, *The Making of the Constitution* 3–54 (Boston: Little, Brown, 1937) and in Hart & Wechsler's fifth edition, 1–19. Some useful context is available in Michael G. Collins, "Article III Cases, State Courts Duties, and the Madisonian Compromise," 1995 *Wis. L. Rev*. 35. A particularly interesting point of view is that of Akil Reed Amar, *America's Constitution: A Biography* (New York: Random House, 2005). Amar encourages us not to overemphasize the importance of the judiciary branch to the Framers' deliberations. He suggests that the subsequent role of the Supreme Court in our constitutional history may lead us to make too much of the discussions of Article III in Philadelphia. An excellent and thorough discussion of the ratification debates for Article III may be found in Robert N. Clinton, "A Mandatory View of Federal Court Jurisdiction: A Guided Quest for the Original Understanding of Article III," 132 *U. Pa. L. Rev*. 741 (1984) (please note that you do not have to accept Clinton's conclusion to profit from his careful review of the ratification process).

The Judiciary Act of 1789. The received wisdom gives great importance to what the First Congress did to implement Article III. Whether these measures should play an important role in constitutional interpretation is clearly dissected in Maeva Marcus and Natalie Wexler's "The Judiciary Act of 1789: Political Compromise or Constitutional Interpretation?" in *Origins of the Federal Judiciary: Essays on the Judiciary Act of 1789* 13 (New York: Oxford University Press, Maeva Marcus ed., 1992). The essay by Gerhard Casper, "The Judiciary Act of 1789 and Judicial Independence," also in *Origins of the Federal Judiciary* 281, is an interesting treatment of the 1789 Act on a grand scale, placing it as one of the major documents of constitutionalism. An alternate treatment by David Currie, in *The Constitution in Congress: The Federalist Period 1789–1801* (Chicago: University of Chicago Press, 1997), seems to put the 1789 Act in a smaller but still important role, as part of the practical business of getting the new government up and running.

The most important modern debate about the Judiciary Act is its relation to the question of a federal common law. The modern view, expressed in Charles Warren, "New Light on the History of the Federal Judiciary Act of 1789," 37 *Harv. L. Rev. 49* (1923), is that the Act meant for state common law rules to apply in diversity cases. This view is challenged by an intricate historical argument in Wilfrid J. Ritz, *Rewriting the History of the Judiciary Act of 1789: Exposing Myths, Challenging Premises, and Using New Evidence* (Norman, OK: University of Oklahoma Press, Wythe Holt and L. H. LaRue eds., 1990).

PART II: ANALYSIS

Taking Jurisdiction Which Is Given

One could spend (and in this author's opinion mostly waste) two or three years in reading the several hundred law review articles devoted to this most glamorous of federal jurisdiction problems. For sheer intellectual satisfaction, it is hard to match Henry Hart, "The Power of Congress to Limit the Jurisdiction of Federal Courts: An Exercise in Dialectic," 66 *Harv. L. Rev.* 1362 (1953). Beyond that, I will list here a few works that seem to be the best contemporary statement of each point of view. Any one of these works will point to many more references for the dedicated reader. The most straightforward position is that the language of Article III means what it seems to say when it empowers Congress to limit federal court jurisdiction. This point of view is given in historical perspective by Gerald Gunther, "Congressional Power to Curtail Federal Court Jurisdiction: An Opinionated Guide to the Ongoing Debate," 36 *Stan. L. Rev.* 895 (1984). One level of response is that the federal courts have a defined minimum role to play, which cannot be reduced. Lawrence Sager, Foreword: "Constitutional Limitations on Congress' Authority to Regulate the Jurisdiction of the Federal Courts," 95 *Harv. L. Rev.* 17 (1981). Another level of response is that Congress is required to vest all "cases" within Article III (but not "controversies") in some federal court. This theory has been powerfully articulated by Akil Reed Amar in "The Two-Tiered Structure of the Judiciary Act of 1789," 138 *U. Penn. L. Rev.* 1499 (1990), and powerfully criticized by Martin Redish, "Text, Structure, and Common Sense in the Interpretation of Article III," 138 *U. Penn. L. Rev.* 1633 (1990). A final level of response is that some other particular constitutional clauses limit congressional power in the absence of a compelling interest. For one example of this argument, see Laurence H. Tribe, "Jurisdictional Gerrymandering: Zoning Disfavored Rights Out of the Federal Courts," 16 *Harv. Civil Rights—Civil Liberties L. Rev.* 129 (1981). The only case to discuss this question explicitly was *Ex parte* McCardle (1868). Very useful to understanding the inconclusive holding and implications of that case is

William Van Alstyne, "A Critical Guide to *Ex Parte* McCardle," 15 *Ariz. L. Rev.* 229 (1973).

Adding Jurisdiction Which Is Not Given

Questions of federal law. A helpful and clear theoretical explanation of federal question jurisdiction, and an article that has more than once provided the framework for a Supreme Court opinion, is Paul Mishkin, "The Federal 'Question' in the District Courts," 53 *Colum. L. Rev.* 157 (1953). Another good primer is William Cohen, "The Broken Compass: The Requirement That a Case Arise 'Directly' under Federal Law," 115 *U. Penn. L. Rev.* 890 (1967). Mishkin's approach is theoretical and searches for conceptual clarity. Cohen argues that conceptual clarity is impossible and urges a practical analysis. For an updated discussion of these same issues, see John B. Oakley, "Federal Jurisdiction and the Problem of the Litigative Unit: When Does What 'Arise Under' Federal Law," 76 *Tex. L. Rev.* 1829 (1998). A fairly compelling case that the subject is needlessly confused is in Martha Field, "The Uncertain Nature of Federal Jurisdiction," 22 *Wm. & Mary L. Rev.* 683 (1981). David Shapiro takes a different view in "Jurisdiction and Discretion," 60 *N.Y.U.L. Rev.* 543 (1985).

Protective jurisdiction. Mishkin's general article in the preceding paragraph is a good introduction to the issue of protective jurisdiction. For a discussion reflecting recent cases and modern problems, a good choice is Eric J. Segall, "Article III as a Grant of Power: Protective Jurisdiction, Federalism and the Federal Courts," 54 *Fla. L. Rev.* 361 (2002).

The Boundaries of a Case (or Controversy)

Standing. Once upon a time, the law of standing seemed to be a fixed, technical set of rules, serving to constrain the discretion of courts. The best evocation of that era is found in the history recounted by Steven L. Winter, "The Metaphor of Standing and the Problem of Self-Governance," 40 *Stan. L. Rev.* 1371 (1988). A profound review of the evolution of standing law can be found in Joseph G. Vining, *Legal Identity: The Coming of Age of Public Law* (New Haven: Yale, 1978). For a penetrating contemporary analysis, see Cass R. Sunstein, "Standing and the Privatization of Public Law," 88 *Colum. L. Rev.* 1432 (1988). Among scholars calling directly for abolition of standing doctrine, the most influential article is probably William A. Fletcher, "The Structure of Standing," 98 *Yale L.J.* 221 (1988). So far, the scholarly literature attacking standing doctrine has been ignored by the courts.

Supplemental jurisdiction. For an historical overview, see Mary B. McManamon, "Dispelling the Myths of Pendent and Ancillary Jurisdiction: The Ramifications of a Revised History," 46 *Wash. & Lee L. Rev.* 863 (1989). There is an organized and elegant explanation of the general principles involved in Richard A. Matasar, "A Pendent and Ancillary Jurisdiction Primer: The Scope and Limits of Supplemental Jurisdiction," 17 *U.C. Davis L. Rev.* 103 (1983). There is a cogent explanation of how Congress, with the best of intentions, made a mess of this whole corner of the law in Richard D. Freer, "Compounding Confusion and Hampering Diversity: Life After *Finley* and the Supplemental Jurisdiction Statute," 40 *Emory L. Rev.* 445 (1991).

Section 2 as a Structure of Federalism

Adequate state grounds. For a general description of the doctrine and its historical foundation, see Alfred Hill, "The Inadequate State Ground," 65 *Colum. L. Rev.* 943 (1965). In recent years, scholars have increasingly suggested that the adequate state ground doctrine should be abandoned. An excellent survey of these arguments is Richard Matasar and Gregory Bruch, "Procedural Common Law, Federal Jurisdictional Policy, and Abandonment of the Adequate and Independent State Grounds Doctrine," 86 *Colum. L. Rev.* 1291 (1986). For a strong rebuttal of this point of view, see Cynthia L. Fountaine, "Article III and the Adequate and Independent State Grounds Doctrine," 48 *Am. U.L. Rev.* 1053 (1999).

The Parity of State Courts

Habeas corpus. An excellent source on the history of the writ in America is William F. Duker, *A Constitutional History of Habeas Corpus* (Westport, CT: Greenwood, 1980). A classic article on the underlying constitutional issues, coupled with a contemporary critique of the Warren Court, is Paul Bator, "Finality in Criminal Law and Federal Habeas Corpus for State Prisoners," 76 *Harv. L. Rev.* 441 (1963). Conversely, a nice critique of the Burger Court's retreat from Warren Court precedents appears in Louis M. Seidman, "Factual Guilt and the Burger Court: An Examination of Continuity and Change in Criminal Procedure," 80 *Colum. L. Rev.* 436 (1980). A good review of the cases in the 1980s is Joseph L. Hoffmann, "The Supreme Court's New Vision of Federal Habeas Corpus for State Prisoners," 1989 *Sup. Ct. Rev.* 165. The 1996 statutes are reviewed in Daniel J. Meltzer, "Congress, Courts, and Constitutional Remedies," 86 *Geo. L.J.* 2537 (1998).

Federal civil rights suits. The standard reference for lawyers and trial-court judges is Martin A. Schwartz, *Section 1983 Litigation: Claims, Defenses, and Fees* (New York: Wiley, 3d ed., 1997). Whether Monroe v. Pape (1961) was a vindication of history or a twisted rendition has been the subject of a lively controversy. Eric H. Zagrans, "'Under Color of *What* Law: A Reconstructed Model of § 1983 Liability," 71 *Va. L. Rev.* 499 (1985), charges that the opinion distorts the statutory meaning, whereas

Steven L. Winter, "The Meaning of 'Under Color of' Law," 91 *Mich. L. Rev.* 323 (1992), reaches the opposite conclusion.

Social Change and Diversity Jurisdiction

There is an astonishingly complete and reflective review of both the policies of diversity jurisdiction and its technical rules in David P. Currie, "The Federal Courts and the American Law Institute," 36 *U. Chi. L.R.* 1 (1968). If you're only going to read one thing about diversity, this should be it. A more recent account of the underlying policy dispute, opposing diversity jurisdiction in a balanced argument, is Larry Kramer, "Diversity Jurisdiction," 1990 *B.Y.U. L Rev.* 97. There is a brief but excellent treatment of the current legal issues in Erwin Chemerinsky, *Federal Jurisdiction* 288–310 (New York: Aspen, 4th ed., 2003). One of the twentieth century's most distinguished federal judges has surveyed the early history in Henry J. Friendly, "The Historical Basis of Diversity Jurisdiction," 41 *Harv. L. Rev.* 483 (1928).

The Federal Common Law

In diversity cases. I think the best law review article ever written on any subject is John Hart Ely, "The Irrepressible Myth of *Erie*," 87 *Harv. L. Rev.* 693 (1974). Ely sees the main justification for *Erie* in ideas of federalism, that the courts should not be able to supply law that Congress lacked the power to make. Paul Mishkin, "Some Further Last Words on *Erie*—The Thread," 87 *Harv. L. Rev.* 1682 (1974), sees separation of powers as the dominant value, arguing that Congress could in fact do much more than the courts can. William Casto, "The *Erie* Doctrine and the Structure of Constitutional Revolutions," 62 *Tulane L. Rev.* 97 (1988), places greater significance on the natural law versus positivism argument central to this volume's treatment of the subject. See, generally, Edward A. Purcell, Jr., *Brandeis and the Progressive Constitution:* Erie, *the Judicial Power, and the Politics of the Federal Courts in Twentieth-Century America* (New Haven: Yale, 2000).

In federal question cases. For a theoretical overview, see Martha A. Field, "Sources of Law: The Scope of Federal Common Law," 99 *Harv. L. Rev.* 881 (1986). For a historical account, see William A. Fletcher, "The General Common Law and Section 34 of the Judiciary Act of 1789: The Example of Marine Insurance," 97 *Harv. L. Rev.* 1513 (1984). For a balanced and authoritative general statement, see Henry J. Friendly, "In Praise of *Erie*—and of the New Federal Common Law," 39 *N.Y.U.L. Rev* 383 (1964).

Cases Arising under the Constitution

An influential article, written shortly after *Bivens*, did much to shape the early dialogue. Walter E. Dellinger, "Of Rights and Remedies: The

Constitution as a Sword," 85 *Harv. L. Rev.* 1532 (1972). The cases seeming to retreat from *Bivens* are analyzed quite unfavorably in Joan Steinman, "Backing Off *Bivens* and the Ramifications of this Retreat for the Vindication of First Amendment Rights," 83 *Mich. L. Rev.* 269 (1984).

Implied Statutory Causes of Action

There is one penetrating analysis of implied causes of action in the context of the modern administrative state, that is, Richard Stewart and Cass Sunstein, "Public Programs and Private Rights," 95 *Harv. L. Rev.* 1191 (1982). Beyond that, analyses mainly cover pros and cons. In favor of the earlier willingness to infer causes of action, and analyzing recent cases critically, see Susan J. Stabile, "The Role of Congressional Intent in Determining the Existence of Implied Private Rights of Action," 71 *Notre Dame L. Rev.* 861 (1996). Taking the opposite position is George D. Brown, "Of Activism and *Erie*—Implication Doctrine's Implications for the Nature and Role of the Federal Courts," 69 *Iowa L. Rev.* 617 (1984).

Courts outside Article III

The best overview of the courts outside Article III is Paul Bator, "The Constitution as Architecture: Legislative and Administrative Courts under Article III," 65 *Ind. L.J.* 233 (1990). The most thought-provoking discussion is Judith Resnick, "The Mythic Meaning of Article III," 56 *U. Colo. L. Rev.* 581 (1985). A good discussion of the specific situation in bankruptcy is Lawrence K. Snider, Louis P. Rochkind, Jonathan S. Green, Leslie Stein, and Jay L. Welford, "The Bankruptcy Amendments and Federal Judgeship Act of 1984," 83 *Mich. L. Rev.* 775 (1984).

Table of Cases

A

Air Courier Conference v. APWU, 498 U.S. 517 (1991)
Alexander v. Sandoval, 532 U.S. 275 (2001)
Allen v. McCurry, 449 U.S. 90 (1980)
Allen v. Wright, 468 U.S. 737 (1984)
American Ins. Co. v. Canter, 26 U.S. (1 Pet.) 511 (1828)
Anderson v. Creighton, 483 U.S. 635 (1987)

B

Baltimore & Ohio Railroad v. Baugh, 149 U.S. 368 (1893)
Bank of United States v. Deveaux, 9 U.S. (5 Cranch) 61, 87 (1809)
Barrows v. Jackson, 346 U.S. 249 (1953)
Bivens v. Six Unknown Named Agents of Federal Bureau of Narcotics, 403 U.S. 388 (1971)
Black & White Taxicab & Transfer Co. v. Brown & Yellow Taxicab Co., 276 U.S. 518, 524 (1928)
Bob Jones University v. United States, 461 U.S. 574 (1983)
Brown v. Allen, 344 U.S. 443 (1953)
Bush v. Gore, 531 U.S. 98 (2000)
Bush v. Lucas, 462 U.S. 367 (1983)

C

Cannon v. University of Chicago, 441 U.S 677 (1979)
Carafas v. LaVallee, 391 U.S. 234 (1968)
Carden v. Arkoma Associates, 494 U.S. 185 (1990)
Carlson v. Green, 446 U.S. 14, 51 (1980) (Rehnquist, J., dissenting)
Chappell v. Wallace, 462 U.S. 296 (1983)
City of Chicago v. International College of Surgeons, 118 S.Ct. 523, 533–34 (1997)
City of Dawson v. Columbia Ave. Sav. Fund, 197 U.S. 178, 180 (1905)
City of Indianapolis v. Chase National Bank (1941)
Clemons v. Mississippi, 494 U.S. 738 (1990)
Cort v. Ash, 422 U.S. 66 (1975)
Craig v. Boren, 429 U.S. 190 (1976)
Crowell v. Benson, 285 U.S. 22 (1932)

D

Daniels v. Allen, 344 U.S. 443 (1953)
Data Processing Services Organizations v. Camp, 397 U.S. 150 (1970)
Davis v. Passman, 442 U.S. 228 (1979)
D.C. Court of Appeals v. Feldman, 460 U.S. 462 (1983)
DeShaney v. Winnebago County Dep't of Soc. Servs., 489 U.S. 189 (1989)
Dickerson v. United States, 530 U.S. 428 (2000)

E

Elk Grove Unified School District v. Newdow, 124 S. Ct. 2301(2004)
Erie Railroad v. Tompkins, 304 U.S. 64 (1938)
Evra Corp. v. Swiss Bank Corp., 673 F.2d 951 (7th Cir. 1982)
Ex parte Bakelite Corp., 279 U.S. 438 (1929)
Ex parte McCardle, 73 U.S. 318 (1868)
Ex parte Royall, 117 U.S. 241 (1886)
Ex parte Young, 209 U.S. 123 (1908)

F

Fay v. Noia, 372 U.S. 391 (1963)
Federal Election Commission v. Akins, 524 U.S. 11 (1998)
Felker v. Turpin, 518 U.S. 651, 664 (1996)
Filartiga v. Pena Irala, 630 F.2d 876 (2d. Cir. 1980)
Finley v. United States, 490 U.S. 545 (1989)
Frank v. Mangum, 237 U.S. 309 (1915)
Freeman v. Howe, 65 U.S. 450 (1860)

G

Glidden Co. v. Zdanok, 370 U.S. 539 (1962)

H

Hamdan v. Rumsfield, 126 S. Ct. 2749 (2006)
Harlow v. Fitzgerald, 457 U.S. 800, 818 (1982)
Hendry v. Moore, 318 U.S. 133 (1943)
Henry v. Mississippi, 379 U.S. 443 (1965)
Hensley v. Municipal Court, 371 U.S. 236 (1973)
Hepburn & Dundas v. Ellzey, 6 U.S. (2 Cranch) 445 (1805).
Herb v. Pitcairn, 324 U.S. 117, 125–26 (1945)
Hope v. Pelzer, 536 U.S. 730, 739-41 (2002)
Hudson v. Palmer, 468 U.S. 517 (1984)
Hurn v. Oursler, 289 U.S. 238 (1933)

I

In re Broaderick's Will, 88 U.S. (21 Wall.) 503 (1875)
In re Burrus, 136 U.S. 586, 593–94 (1890)
Indiana *ex rel.* Anderson v. Brand, 303 U.S. 95 (1938)

J

J.I. Case Co. v. Borak, 377 U.S. 426 (1964)
Jones v. Cunningham, 371 U.S. 236 (1963)

K

Kaufman v. United States, 394 U.S. 217, 226 (1969)
Kerney v. Fort Griffin Fandangle Assn., 624 F.2d 717 (5th Cir. 1980)
Kramer v. Caribbean Mills, Inc., 394 U.S. 823 (1969)
Kremer v. Chemical Construction Corporation, 456 U.S. 461 (1982)
Kuhn v. Fairmont Coal Co., 215 U.S. 349 (1910)

L

Lane v. Williams, 455 U.S. 624 (1982)
Lugar v. Edmondson Oil Co., 457 U.S. 922, 929 (1982)
Lumbermen's Mutual Casualty Co. v. Elbert, 348 U.S. 48 (1954)
Lujan v. Defenders of Wildlife, 504 U.S. 555 (1992)

M

Mapp v. Ohio, 367 U.S. 643 (1961)
Marbury v. Madison, 5 U.S. 137 (1803)
Markham, Allen Property Custodian v. Allen, 326 U.S. 490 (1945)
Massaro v. United States, 538 U.S. 500 (2003)
Massiah v. United States, 377 U.S. 201 (1964)
Martin v. Hunter's Lessee, 14 U.S. 304 (1816)
Maynard v. Cartwright, 486 U.S. 356 (1988)
McCleskey v. Zant, 499 U.S. 467 (1991)
McCulloch v. Maryland, 17 U.S. 316 (1819)
Michigan v. Long, 463 U.S. 1032 (1983)
Mitchum v. Foster, 407 U.S. 225, 242 (1972)
Miranda v. Arizona, 384 U.S. 436 (1966).
Monell v. Dep't of Soc. Servs., 436 U.S. 658 (1978)
Monroe v. Pape, 365 U.S. 167 (1961)
Moore v. Dempsey, 261 U.S. 86 (1923)
Moore v. New York Cotton Exchange, 270 U.S. 593 (1926)
Murdock v. City of Memphis, 87 U.S. 590 (1875)
Murray v. Carrier, 477 U.S. 478 (1986)
Murray's Lessee v. Hoboken Land & Improvement Co., 59 U.S. 272 (1856)

N

NAACP v. Alabama *ex rel.* Flowers, 377 U.S. 288 (1964)
NAACP v. Alabama *ex rel.* Patterson, 357 U.S. 449 (1958)
National Mutual Insurance Co. v. Tidewater Transfer Co., Inc., 337 U.S. 582 (1949)
Navarro Savings v. Lee, 446 U.S. 458 (1980)
New York Times v. Sullivan, 376 U.S. 254 (1964)
Northern Pipeline Construction Co. v. Marathon Pipe Line Co., 458 U.S. 50 (1982)

O

O'Callahan v. Parker, 395 U.S. 258, 264 (1969)
O'Donoghue v. United States, 289 U.S. 516 (1933)
Osborn v. Bank of the United States, 22 U.S. 738 (1824)
Owen Equipment & Erection Co. v. Kroger (1978)

P

Palmore v. United States, 411 U.S. 389 (1973)
Parratt v. Taylor, 451 U.S. 527 (1981)
Paul v. Davis, 424 U.S. 693 (1976)
Peyton v. Rowe, 391 U.S. 54 (1968)
Pierce v. Society of Sisters, 268 U.S. 510 (1925)
Preiser v. Rodriguez, 411 U.S. 475 (1973)

Q

Quern v. Jordan, 440 U.S. 332 (1979)

R

Rooker v. Fidelity Trust Co., 263 U.S. 413 (1923)
Rose v. Lundy, 455 U.S. 509 (1982)
Runyon v. McCrary, 427 U.S. 160 (1976)

S

Saadeh v. Farouki, 107 F.3d 52 (D.C. Cir. 1997)
Sanders v. United States, 373 U.S. 1 (1963)
Sawyer v. Whitley, 505 U.S. 333, 336 (1992)
Scheuer v. Rhodes, 416 U.S. 232, 240 (1974)
Schlup v. Delo, 513 U.S. 298, 327 (1995)
Schweiker v. Chilicky, 487 U.S. 412 (1988)
Shelley v. Kraemer, 334 U.S. 1 (1948)
Siegert v. Gilley, 500 U.S. 226 (1991)
Siler v. Louisville & Nashville Railroad, 213 U.S. 175 (1909)
Singleton v. Wulff, 428 U.S. 106 (1976)
Slack v. McDaniel, 529 U.S. 473 (2000)
Sosa v. Alvarez Machain, 542 U.S. 692 (2004)
Standard Oil Company of California v. Johnson, 316 U.S. 481 (1942)
State *ex rel.* Anderson v. Brand, 13 N.E.2d 955 (Ind. 1938)
State Farm Fire & Casualty Co. v. Tashire (1967)
Stone v. Powell, 428 U.S. 465 (1976)
Strawbridge v. Curtiss, 7 U.S. 267 (1806)
Steigleder v. McQuesten, 198 U.S. 141 (1905)
Strickler v. Greene, 527 U.S. 263 (1999)
Stringer v. Black, 503 U.S. 222 (1992)
Swift v. Tyson, 41 U.S. 1 (1842)

T

Teague v. Lane, 489 U.S. 288 (1989)
Terry v. Ohio, 392 U.S. 1 (1968)
Textile Workers v. Lincoln Mills, 353 U.S. 448 (1957)
Touche Ross & Co. v. Redington, 442 U.S. 560 (1979)
Trest v. Cain, 522 U.S. 87 (1997)

U

United Mine Workers v. Gibbs, 383 U.S. 715 (1966)
United States v. Darby, 312 U.S. 100, 124 (1941)

United States v. Kimball Foods, Inc., 440 U.S. 715 (1979)
United States v. Little Lake Misere Land Co., 412 U.S. 580 (1973)
United States v. Stanley, 483 U.S. 669 (1987)
United States v. Will, 449 U.S. 200, 217–218 (1980)
United Steelworkers v. R.H. Bouligny, Inc., 382 U.S. 145 (1965)

V

Verlinden B. V. v. Central Bank of Nigeria, 461 U.S. 480 (1983)
Vermont Agency of Natural Resources v. United States, 529 U.S. 765 (2000)

W

Wainwright v. Sykes, 433 U.S. 72 (1977)
Webster v. Doe, 486 U.S. 592 (1988)
Will v. Michigan Department of State Police, 491 U.S. 58 (1989)
Williams v. Georgia, 349 U.S. 375 (1955)
Williams v. United States, 289 U.S. 553 (1933)
Wright v. Georgia, 373 U.S. 284 (1963)

Y

Younger v. Harris, 401 U.S. 37 (1971)

Index

About the Author

PATRICK BAUDE is Fuchs Professor of Law at Indiana University, Bloomington, where he has taught constitutional law since 1968. He has also taught at the University of Illinois, the University of Paris, and Warsaw University. His research involves various aspects of federalism, focused on federal courts and state constitutions. He has also been special counsel to the Governor of Indiana and President of the Indiana Board of Law Examiners. He holds a J.D. from the University of Kansas and a Master of Law from Harvard.

www.ingramcontent.com/pod-product-compliance
Ingram Content Group UK Ltd.
Pitfield, Milton Keynes, MK11 3LW, UK
UKHW020821290926
15470UKWH00003B/1301

9 780313 312045